Schluß mit typischen Englisch-Fehlern!

humboldt
Sprachen

Ihre erworbenen Sprachkenntnisse können Sie mit folgenden Titeln aus unserem Programm gezielt ausbauen:

Englisch in 30 Tagen	ht 11
Englisch für Fortgeschrittene	ht 61
Englisch – Bild für Bild	ht 296
Englischer Basis-Wortschatz	ht 574
Englisch – jetzt in Comics	ht 578
Englische Grammatik	ht 617
Französisch in 30 Tagen	ht 40
Französisch für Fortgeschrittene	ht 109
Französisch – Bild für Bild	ht 297
Französisch – jetzt in Comics	ht 579
Spanisch in 30 Tagen	ht 57
Spanisch – Bild für Bild	ht 345
Spanisch – jetzt in Comics	ht 581
Spanisch für Fortgeschrittene	ht 626
Italienisch in 30 Tagen	ht 55
Italienisch für Fortgeschrittene	ht 108
Italienisch – Bild für Bild	ht 344
Italienisch – jetzt in Comics	ht 580
Russisch in 20 Lektionen	ht 81
Dänisch in 30 Tagen	ht 124
Griechisch für den Urlaub	ht 699
Griechisch – jetzt in Comics	ht 652
Türkisch für den Urlaub	ht 628

Acht Titel dieser Liste gibt es auch als Sprachkurse mit Audiocassetten, nämlich:

Englisch in 30 Tagen	ht 800
Französisch in 30 Tagen	ht 801
Italienisch in 30 Tagen	ht 802
Spanisch in 30 Tagen	ht 803
Türkisch für den Urlaub	ht 804
Englisch für Fortgeschrittene	ht 805
Spanisch für Fortgeschrittene	ht 806
Griechisch für den Urlaub	ht 808

Schluß mit typischen Englisch-Fehlern!

Von Dr. Sonia Brough und
Carolyn Kilday Wittmann

humboldt

humboldt-taschenbuch 664

Umschlaggestaltung: Christa Manner, München
unter Verwendung einer Zeichnung
von Margarethe Braun, Ingolstadt

Zeichnungen im Innenteil: Alfred Taubenberger

Hinweis für den Leser:

Die im Text verwendeten Symbole haben folgende Bedeutung:

 Wo dieses Symbol erscheint, soll Ihnen ein Licht aufgehen. Es weist auf eine „Eselsbrücke" hin, die Ihnen helfen soll, sich etwas Wichtiges zu merken.

 Dieses Warndreieck bedeutet „Vorsicht!". Hier wird auf eine besonders tückische Fehlerquelle hingewiesen, auf die Sie achtgeben sollten.

 Dieser entsetzte „Smiley" erscheint hin und wieder, wenn Helmut, einer der Hauptdarsteller in diesem Buch, einen gravierenden Englisch-Fehler begangen hat. Sie sollten Helmut in solchen Fällen tunlichst nicht nachahmen!

Abkürzungen

Am.	amerikanisch	*o.s.*	oneself
Brit.	britisch	*pl.*	Plural, Mehrzahl
bes.	besonders	*s.o.*	someone
bzw.	beziehungsweise	*s.th.*	something
jd.	jemand(en)	*umgs.*	umgangssprachlich
jdm.	jemandem	*usw.*	und so weiter
jds.	jemandes	*vgl.*	vergleiche

© 1991 by Humboldt-Taschenbuchverlag Jacobi KG, München
Druck: Presse-Druck Augsburg
Printed in Germany

ISBN 3-581-66664-2

Inhalt

Vorwort 6

Hauptteil 9

Britisch versus Amerikanisch 141

„Falsche Freunde" 145

Schlüssel zu den Übungen 153

Register 157

Vorwort

Da fehlen einem doch glatt die Worte! Hat man mit Müh und Not jede Menge Wortschatz eingepaukt, greift man doch immer wieder in die falsche Schublade: Diese verflixten deutschen Wörter, die im Englischen zwei, drei, vier oder noch mehr Entsprechungen haben. „Platz", zum Beispiel. Heißt das nun *room*, *space* oder *place*, oder aber *seat*, wenn nicht gar *square*? Ganz schön verwirrend, nicht wahr?

Aber mit diesem Buch werden Sie sich schnell wieder zurechtfinden. Das richtige Wort am richtigen Platz – pardon, an der richtigen Stelle – das ist unser Ziel. Wie wichtig das ist, dies weiß auch längst unser „Hauptdarsteller" Helmut, dem wir noch mehrmals begegnen werden. Helmut stammt aus Deutschland und hat sich wieder einmal bei der Familie Wilson in London eingenistet, um sein Englisch auf Vordermann zu bringen. Da er sich das in der gleichen Reihe erschienene Buch *Englische Grammatik – kurz und schmerzlos** längst einverleibt hat, ist er eigentlich schon recht „grammatikfest"; nur hapert es noch hin und wieder am Wortschatz. Wir werden die Qual der Wahl dieses charmanten jungen Mannes öfter miterleben – und einiges daraus lernen . . .

Kurz zum Aufbau des Buches: Jedes Stichwortkapitel besteht aus drei Teilen:

① Eine Anekdote oder illustrierte Beispielsätze, in denen die kniffligen Wörter vorgestellt werden.

② Ein fettumrandetes Kästchen, in dem diese Wörter unter die Lupe genommen werden. Hierbei helfen wiederum typische Beispielsätze sowie auch Eselsbrücken.

---

* Bd. 617; Humboldt-Taschenbuchverlag

③ Zur Abrundung ein kleiner Test mit ganz typischen Anwendungsbeispielen, mit deren Hilfe Sie Ihre soeben erworbenen Kenntnisse überprüfen und festigen können.

Wir raten Ihnen, beim Durcharbeiten der Kästchen immer wieder auf den Ausgangstext zurückzublicken, um sich mit den jeweiligen Begriffen vertraut zu machen. Beim Test sollten Sie dann ruhig sowohl das Kästchen als auch den Text zu Rate ziehen. Durch das Zusammenspiel dieser drei Bestandteile werden Sie auf amüsant-anschauliche Weise sicher ans Ziel geführt – treffsichere Wortwahl statt Qual der Wahl mit womöglich peinlichen Fehltritten... Zur Wiederholung können Sie dann nach Lust und Laune zwischen den Kästchen hin und her hüpfen, sozusagen von Wortschatzinsel zu Wortschatzinsel. Dabei dürfen Sie sich natürlich zur Erfrischung auch immer wieder einen Sprung in die Anekdoten und Tests genehmigen.

Übrigens: Wir haben auch viele der behandelten Wörter an anderen Stellen „hineingeschmuggelt", um deren Gebrauch noch mehr zu festigen. Darüber hinaus werden Sie auf jede Menge aktuelles Vokabular stoßen und somit Ihren Wortschatz noch mehr erweitern.

Die Auswahl der Problemfälle ist natürlich nicht erschöpfend. Wir haben ganz gezielt eine Reihe von Begriffen ausgesucht, mit denen gerade Deutschsprachige ihre Schwierigkeiten haben. Um Ihnen jeweils das Kernproblem vor Augen zu halten, haben wir dann und wann eine vereinfachte Darstellung gerne in Kauf genommen.

Ein Tip noch: Obwohl Lernbuch, hat es das Zeug, Sie zu fesseln. Galoppieren Sie es daher möglichst nicht in einem Zug durch, da sonst unterwegs wieder vieles verlorenginge. Schnuppern Sie das Buch ruhig ein bißchen nach Wörtern ab, die Ihnen spontan zusagen. Besser jeden Tag ein halbes Stündchen als eine lange Wochenendorgie – das bringt wesentlich mehr. Und vergessen Sie nicht: Es ist nicht mit einem Mal getan – beim Sprachenlernen liegt in der **Wiederholung** der Schlüssel zum Erfolg.

Wir wünschen Ihnen dabei viel Spaß!

Autoren und Verlag

Hauptteil

aufstehen

get up?   stand up?

*Helmut always **gets up** late when he's in England.*

*Being a gentleman, Helmut **stood up** to give Sally his seat.*

---

aus dem <u>Bett</u> aufstehen (und sich fertig machen):

get up

- kann <u>nicht</u> durch *stand up* ersetzt werden

---

sich vom Stuhl, Sofa usw. <u>erheben</u>:

stand up

- kann auch mit ***get up*** ausgedrückt werden

Im Zweifel nehmen Sie ***get up***, denn das deckt beide Fälle ab. Wenn ***from*** + „Sitzgelegenheit" folgt, **muß** man sogar ***get up*** nehmen:

*He **got up from the sofa** straightaway.*

stand up wird eher in formellen Situationen bevorzugt:

The class stood up as the headmistress came in.

Und falls Sie nach dem „Aufstehen" noch nicht ganz munter sein sollten, hier ein kleiner Test:

---

get up oder *stand up*? Setzen Sie die passende Form ein.

1. If you _____ now, you might get some breakfast before it's all gone.

2. In British cinemas most people don't _____ for the national anthem any more.

Bank

bank?   bench?

This is probably the nearest Fred will ever get to a <u>bank account</u> – sleeping on an uncomfortable <u>bench</u> in front of the <u>bank</u>. You may feel sorry for him, but actually he's happier here than he was in prison a few months ago, slaving away at a <u>work bench</u>. But he'd better be careful, otherwise he might appear before the <u>magistrate's bench</u> again, and that would be the end of his life in the open.

---

work bench – Werkbank   **appear before the magistrate's bench** – vor den Kadi („die Richterbank") kommen

bank	Geldinstitut

I've just opened a savings account at Lloyd's Bank in the High Street.

bank holiday – gesetzlicher Feiertag (an dem in erster Linie die Banken geschlossen bleiben)

bench   Sitzbank, auch übertragen in Verbindung mit verschiedenen Berufen

substitutes' bench – Reservebank
backbencher – Hinterbänkler

After jogging for an hour he was glad to have a rest on the park bench.

It often takes years for young MPs to make their way from the back to the front benches.

---

bank oder *bench*?

1. It can be very frustrating for a footballer to have to sit on the substitutes' _____ for weeks on end.

2. If you need traveller's cheques, you'd better order them at the _____ soon.

3. Ever since Parliament allowed television to broadcast debates, there has been less newspaper-reading and falling asleep on the back _____ (*pl.*).

bemerken

notice?   remark?

*I couldn't help **noticing** that he had odd socks on.*

*I **remarked** that I liked his shoes very much.*

notice	mit den <u>Augen</u>/<u>Ohren</u> usw. bemerken, wahrnehmen
	I noticed – mir ist aufgefallen
	Did you notice that funny notice on the noticeboard?
remark	(gehoben) <u>mündlich</u> bemerken, sagen
	She remarked how much she liked my new curtains.
	Statt des gehobenen *remark* sagt man meist ganz einfach ***say***.
	re<u>mark</u> mit dem <u>**Mund**</u>, sonst ***notice***

---

notice – Anschlag   ***notice-board*** – schwarzes Brett

---

notice oder *remark*? Setzen Sie die passende Form ein.

When she _____ me slipping in through the door half an hour late, she loudly _____ that she was a great believer in punctuality.

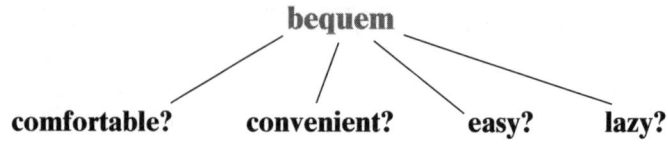

The easy way out

The nearest shops to my house are over a mile away, so it's either a question of putting on <u>a comfortable pair of shoes</u> and walking half an hour to the shopping centre, or taking <u>the easy way out</u> and using the car. In time, of course, you get very <u>lazy</u> and fill your freezer and pantry with convenience foods. I do draw the line at TV dinners, however. It may be <u>convenient</u> to sit back in <u>a comfortable armchair</u> eating a meal which took you three minutes to heat up in the microwave, but I must admit even my dog turned his nose up at the lasagna I offered to share with him during "Dallas" the other evening.

comfortable	bequem, was das körperliche Wohlbefinden angeht
	I wish we had more comfortable chairs to sit on in the office.
convenient	sehr praktisch, keine Umstände verursachend
	It's so convenient living in the town centre with so many shops and restaurants nearby.
easy	einfach, mühelos, ohne viel körperlichen oder geistigen Aufwand
	He's made life very easy for himself by just sending his children to boarding school.
lazy	faul, bequem
	Sometimes he's too lazy to get up and answer the phone.

comfortable, convenient, easy oder *lazy?*

1. The new flat's very _____ as far as public transport goes – there are bus stops and a Tube station just down the road.

2. Sit down and make yourself _____ .

3. I know everybody thinks that civil servants are _____ and lead a very _____ life. They ought to try my job at the Department of the Environment.

4. As Margaret says, there are no _____ solutions to difficult problems.

---

civil servant – Beamter   ***Department of the Environment*** – Umweltministerium

besondere(r,-s)

special? particular?

A special occasion

Mr Wilson: *As it's your birthday, I've decided to give you a <u>special treat</u> and take you out for a meal and then to the cinema. Is there <u>any particular film</u> you'd like to see?*

Mrs Wilson: *It's not like you to be so generous, Norman. Are you making a <u>special effort</u> because you forgot our wedding anniversary last month?*

Mr Wilson: *No, there's no <u>particular reason</u> – except that you're a very <u>special person</u> ...*

---

give s.o. a special treat – jdm. eine besondere Freude machen

Dies ist schon ein besonderer Fall (*a special case*), denn die Unterschiede zwischen *special* und *particular* sind besonders fein (*particularly subtle*) und verlangen daher Ihre besondere Aufmerksamkeit (*your special attention*).

special	**1.** außergewöhnlich, nicht alltäglich, Sonder ...
	a special person/case/event *What's so special about this restaurant?*
	2. speziell, Sonder...
	special training/treatment *a special technique*
particular	(ganz) bestimmte(r,-s) aus einer Reihe von Möglichkeiten; man stellt sich dabei meist etwas ganz Konkretes vor
	"I'm looking for a couch." – "Have you got any particular style in mind?"

---

special oder *particular*?

I want to get Nick something _____ for his eighteenth birthday, and there's one _____ video camera he's keen on. My sister knows a dealer who might give me a _____ price.

---

be keen on – "scharf" sein auf

besuchen

go and see? / (pay s.o. a) visit? go to? / attend?

It's a busy life

Mrs Wilson: *When was the last time you <u>paid your Auntie Flora a visit</u>, Peter?*

Peter: *Oh, Mum, I'm too busy to <u>go and see all these relatives</u>. On Monday evenings I've got sports, and on Tuesdays and Thursdays I <u>go to my Japanese class</u>. Mr Honda says he expects us to <u>attend the course</u> regularly if we want to <u>go to Kyoto University</u> for our year abroad. That just leaves a bit of free time at the weekends for me to see my friends. Anyway, why don't you go and <u>visit</u> Auntie Flora – she is your sister, after all.*

go and see s.o.	(auch ***go to see s.o.***) jd. besuchen
	I must go and see my parents tomorrow.
pay s.o. a visit	jd. besuchen, jdm. einen Besuch abstatten; gehobener als *go and see*
	You really ought to pay poor Mr Trump a visit.
visit s.o.	jd. besuchen, oft auf offizieller Ebene, nach bestimmten Besuchszeiten, oder aus Verpflichtung
	Will you come and visit me when I'm in jail?
go to	(die Schule/Universität, einen Kurs usw.) <u>regelmäßig</u> besuchen
	I go to body-building classes every night.
	Which school did you go to?
attend	1. (an einem Kurs, einer Klasse usw.) teilnehmen; gehobener als *go to*
	Pupils who are unable to attend a class must provide a written excuse.
	2. (gehoben) (eine Schule usw.) besuchen
	Please list all schools and institutions of higher education you have attended.

go and see, visit, go to oder *attend*? Setzen Sie die passende Form ein.

1. Does your little boy still _____ kindergarten?
2. Foreign ministers from all the EC countries are expected to _____ next month's conference.
3. I must _____ my sister this weekend – she's been in bed with an awful cold.
4. The Archbishop of Canterbury is to _____ the Pope in February.

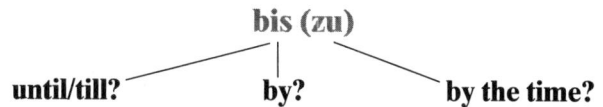

Ups and downs

Mr Wilson: *I wish they'd hurry up. <u>By the time they get us out</u> of this lift the meeting will be over; and I'm supposed to be home <u>by eight at the latest</u> for a dinner party. My wife will kill me if I keep everyone waiting again.*

Mr Smithers: *Well, it's a good thing there's an emergency phone at least. I certainly wouldn't fancy being stuck in this lift with you <u>till tomorrow morning</u>, Mr Wilson.*

Mr Wilson: *If you carry on talking to me in that tone, Smithers, you'll be out of a job <u>by the end of the year</u>.*

---

until/till

werden bei einer ununterbrochenen **Zeitdauer** benutzt; Zustand/Tätigkeit <u>bleiben unverändert</u>

We danced till three o'clock in the morning.

by, by the time

bis <u>spätestens</u>, bis <u>endlich</u>;
beziehen sich auf einen Zeit<u>punkt</u> oder Termin, <u>vor</u> dem etwas geschehen muß(te) usw.

by + Zeitangabe:

*I've got to hand this seminar paper in **by the 28th**.* (Frist/Termin)

*We should have been in Alice Springs **by Friday**.* (Zeitpunkt)

by the time + Verbkonstruktion:

***By the time you've finished** packing, the plane will have left without us.* (Zeitpunkt)

By the time he called *I had left the office.* (Zeitpunkt)

*I want you to be in bed **by the time I get home**.* (Termin)

until 12 o'clock

`----->----->----->----->----->--`

I'll be working until twelve.

```
    ?        ?        ?
  10.30    11.15    11.50    by 12 o'clock!
-----×-----×-----×------------
```

She'll be back by twelve.

Übrigens: *See you later!* – Bis später!

---

until, by oder *by the time?*

1. Could you have the flat cleaned and the dinner ready _____ six o'clock?

2. You're going to stay here _____ you've sobered up.

3. _____ I realized who it was, it was too late to ask for an autograph.

---

sober up – (wieder) nüchtern werden

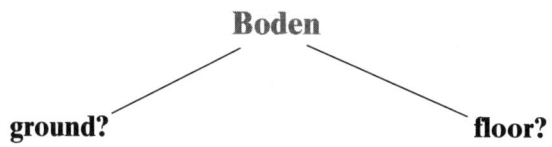

Organic gardening

"What's all this soil doing on my <u>kitchen floor</u>, Jimmy?"

"Well, I'm trying to breed worms, Mum, but if I do it on the <u>ground outside</u> they all crawl away. When I've got enough, I'll put them back into your vegetable bed to make your carrots and cauliflower taste better."

---

organic gardening – biologischer Anbau **breed** – züchten **bed** – Beet
cauliflower – Blumenkohl

Nach diesem tapferen Versuch des Jung-Ökologen Jimmy, wollen wir unsererseits den „Boden" ein bißchen bearbeiten:

---

ground	Boden draußen, Grund
	The ground's so hard, I can hardly get the spade into it.
	We were stuck on the runway for hours before the plane got off the ground.
	Übrigens: ***soil*** – lockerer Boden, Erdreich
floor	Fußboden im Haus
	Why do the kids always leave their toys lying around on the floor?

---

ground oder *floor*?

The _____ is far too wet to let Jimmy and his pals sleep in the tent tonight. We'll just have to spread some mattresses out on the living-room _____ and bed them down there.

---

pal – Freund, „Spezi" **bed s.o. down** – jd. schlafen legen

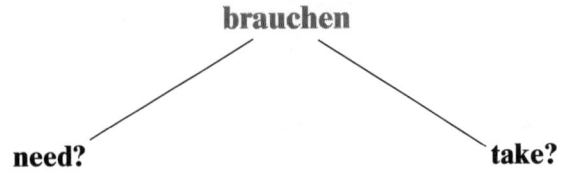

City life

<u>It takes</u> the average commuter up to two hours <u>to</u> get home in the evening rush-hour. At times the traffic almost comes to a standstill. What we <u>need</u> is a more efficient public transport system, or we should introduce more flexible working hours so that everyone isn't travelling to and from work at the same time. I can't understand why <u>it's taking</u> the politicians so long <u>to</u> find a solution to the problem of our congested roads. Perhaps they <u>need</u> a nine-to-five job just to see how the other half lives.

---

commuter – Pendler ***flexible working hours*** – gleitende Arbeitszeit ***congested*** – verstopft ***the other half*** – wir Normalbürger

---

need	benötigen
	This hoover is falling apart – we definitely need a new one.
take	(Zeit, Energie usw.) in Anspruch nehmen, <u>um</u> ein bestimmtes Ziel zu erreichen; betont den <u>Aufwand</u> und wird meist durch ***it*** eingeleitet
	<u>It</u> took him years of hard work to get where he is today.

Übersetzen Sie:

1. Ich brauche eine Krawatte für die Hochzeit.
2. Er braucht nur zehn Minuten, um eine Seite zu tippen.
3. Wie lange hast du gebraucht, um hier herzukommen?

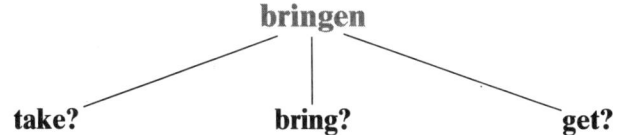

The fun and games are over

If you <u>get</u> me the timetable, we can work out when I have to <u>take</u> you to the station. And don't forget to <u>take</u> your grandmother some flowers when you go to fetch the dog. And another thing, Peter – next time you come home, please don't <u>bring</u> all your friends at the same time.

take	(irgendwo<u>hin</u>)bringen (vom Standort des Sprechers oder Handelnden <u>weg</u>) *Could you take these empty boxes into the cellar?*
bring	<u>her</u>bringen (zum Standort des Sprechers oder Entgegennehmenden <u>her</u>); oft in der Konstruktion *bring s.o. s.th.* *Bring me my slippers, will you?*
get	(her)bringen, <u>holen</u>; meist in der Konstruktion *get s.o. s.th.* *Get him a glass of water, quick!*

take, *bring* oder *get*? Setzen Sie die passende Form ein.

1. The ambulance _____ him straight to hospital, and he was operated on immediately.

2. I'm too lazy to get up – can you _____ me my glasses from the desk?

3. Don't forget to _____ your swimming trunks when you come and see us.

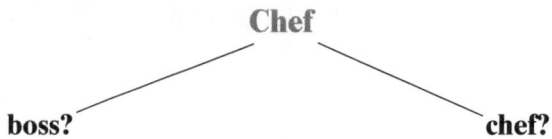

Who's the boss around here?

Sally: *I think you'd make a good chef, Helmut.*
Helmut: *Really?*
Sally: *Well, you're good at planning, you can coordinate things, work under pressure, and you always have everything ready in time.*
Helmut: *Yes, I can just see myself running a huge department in a multinational company...*
Sally: *I said chef, Helmut, not boss. I'm talking about working in a kitchen, not in some big firm. Actually, perhaps you ought to spend less time with your nose in the cooking pots and stick it into your English vocabulary book more often.*
Helmut: *Whatever you say, boss.*

Ist Ihnen klar geworden, was Helmut durcheinandergebracht hat? Das Kästchen gibt Aufschluß.

---

boss	(leicht umgs.) Chef; einen neutralen Allgemeinausdruck für „Chef" gibt es nicht; mögliche Übersetzungen sind:
	head of department, supervisor, manager, managing director usw.
	Wenn die genaue Funktion unbekannt ist, kann man *person in charge* sagen.
	Look out, here comes the boss. We'd better get back to work.
	Übrigens: *boss s.o. around* – jd. herumkommandieren *bossy* – herrisch

chef	<u>Küchen</u>chef, Chef<u>koch</u>
	He says he's chef of a three-star restaurant.
⚠ **chief**	Häuptling
	You look like an Indian chief with all those feathers in your hat.

boss

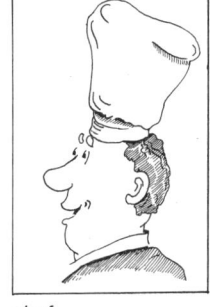
chef

chief

---

boss oder *chef*?

1. My compliments to the _____ – the roast lamb was excellent.

2. The new _____ is starting tomorrow, and everybody in the office is really nervous.

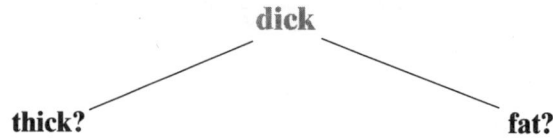

With friends like you, who needs enemies?

One Sunday afternoon Helmut was playing Scrabble with the Wilsons and was collecting quite a lot of points. Just as he was putting down another four-letter word, Sally came in. Helmut knew that she had been trying to lose weight, so he decided to pay her a compliment. "Hello Sally," he said with his usual charming smile, "You're not as thick as you used to be!" ☺ Everyone looked at him, and Sally's brother Peter said very defensively, "Actually, Sally has always been quite clever – in fact, she's probably the most intelligent person in this room." That was when Helmut realized that he must have said something wrong...

Scrabble – „Scrabble", eine Art Wortbildungsspiel

Ja, hier ist unser Helmut voll ins Fettnäpfchen getreten, denn: *thick* bedeutet bei Personen keineswegs „dick", sondern „blöd", „schwer von Begriff". Was er gemeint hat, war natürlich *fat*, aber auch das wäre etwas plump gewesen. Da wäre *plump* (= mollig) schon angebrachter. Aber um Sally ein echtes Kompliment zu machen, hätte er eigentlich sagen müssen: *You're much slimmer than you used to be.* Das Kästchen wird Sie vor ähnlichen „dicken Hunden" bewahren.

fat	dick, fett
	He's almost too fat to get through the front door.
thick	**1.** (Buch, Stoff, Suppe usw.) dick
	This material is too thick for a summer dress.
	2. (sehr umgs.!) blöd, schwer von Begriff
	He must be a bit thick if he can't tell the difference between French and English.

> *thick* oder *fat*?
>
> My wife thinks I'm much too _____, so for my birthday she gave me a _____ book on how to lose weight and an expensive cashmere suit that's three sizes too small for me. She obviously thinks I'm stupid, but I'm not that _____.

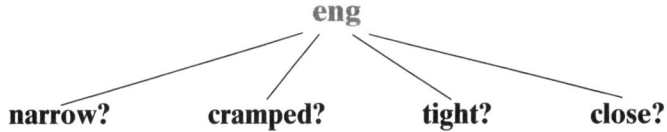

You're cramping my style

Helmut: *Sally, I know you like <u>narrow skirts</u>, but don't you think the one you wore to the party last night was a bit too <u>tight</u>?*

Sally: *Don't be so narrow-minded, Helmut – it's the fashion. I'm more worried about my new shoes. They're such a <u>tight fit</u>, they really hurt.*

Helmut: *I also thought you and John were sitting very <u>close together</u> on the sofa.*

Sally: *I do believe you're jealous, Helmut. The <u>flat</u> was so <u>cramped</u>, there was nowhere else to sit. Anyway, John and I have been <u>close friends</u> for years.*

Helmut: *It's not that I want to cramp your style, but I did take you to the party after all…*

---
cramp someone's style – jd. einengen

Helmut hat wohl die ganze Sache ein bißchen zu eng gesehen. Wir müssen auf jeden Fall etwas in die Breite gehen, um dem breiten Spektrum dieses kleinen Wörtleins gerecht zu werden.

narrow	**1.** schmal, eng (Gegenteil: breit)
	We spent hours walking through the narrow, busy streets and alleyways of the old city.
	2. (im übertragenen Sinn) eng, begrenzt
	He takes a very narrow view of the matter.
	narrow-minded – engstirnig
cramped	räumlich eng, beengend
	He hates cooking in the cramped kitchen.
	Many refugees are living in cramped and filthy conditions.
tight	eng sitzend/anliegend, oft <u>zu</u> eng/fest
	I must have put on weight – these trousers were never so tight before.
close	**1.** ***close to*** – eng an, dicht an/neben
	close together – dicht nebeneinander, eng aneinander
	2. (Beziehungen, Kontakte) eng
	We're still in close contact.

---

narrow, cramped, tight oder *close*?

1. It's so _____ in this flat, there's hardly any room to move.
2. What we need is _____ cooperation between environmentalist groups.
3. Oh Mum, you're a bit behind the times – these jeans are supposed to be _____.
4. She's very _____-minded about foreigners.

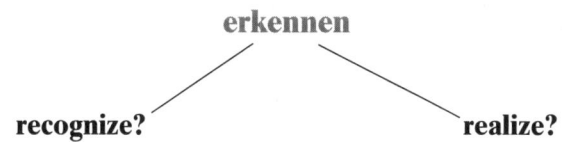

erkennen

recognize?   **realize?**

Fat and happy?

When they told me I had to put on 25 pounds for my role in the new film, I thought it would be great fun. But shortly after I started eating all those fried breakfasts and high-calorie desserts I <u>realized</u> I would have to buy a lot of new clothes. After a month of pigging myself, I looked a different person. When my boyfriend got back from his business tour of the States he hardly <u>recognized me</u>. When he threatened to leave me if I didn't get back down to my normal weight very quickly, I <u>realized</u> that perhaps I had got things slightly out of proportion.

---

pig o.s. – sich den Bauch vollschlagen   **get s.th. out of proportion** – etwas übertreiben

recognize	**1.** wiedererkennen
	I hardly recognized you in those strange glasses.
	2. (sehr gehoben) zur Kenntnis nehmen
	We do recognize the need for reform.
	(wird im Alltagsenglisch relativ selten benutzt)
realize:	***I realized*** – mir wurde klar, mir leuchtete ein
	I soon realized it would be cheaper to rent a flat than to buy one.

---

recognize oder *realize*? Setzen Sie die passende Form ein.

1. I wish they would _____ that they can't learn English unless they make a proper effort.
2. John's smashed the car, I'm afraid. You won't _____ it – it's a complete write-off.

---

make an effort – sich bemühen/anstrengen   ***write-off*** – Totalschaden

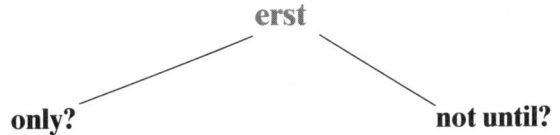

First things first

Sally: *Helmut, you've <u>only</u> written three lines of your English essay so far.*

Helmut: *Yes, but it's <u>only</u> eight o'clock, and I <u>don't</u> have to hand it in <u>until</u> tomorrow afternoon. I'm not really in the mood, anyway. Shall I take you down to the pub for a drink?*

Sally: *<u>Not until</u> you've done at least a page. What's it about, by the way?*

Helmut: *The title is "Are men really more domineering than women?".*

I'm not in the mood – ich habe keine Lust   *domineering* – herrschsüchtig

only	**1.** nur, erst (es ist weniger/früher usw. als erwartet)
	I lent you ten pounds, and you've only given me three back.
	It's only ten past six and we've got the whole evening ahead of us.
	Oft in der Konstruktion *only ... so far*
	We've only interviewed three candidates so far.
	2. nicht eher / nicht früher als; betont den <u>Zeitpunkt</u> (häufig in der <u>Vergangenheit</u>)
	I only got back on Wednesday.
not until	nicht eher / nicht früher als, nicht (be)vor; betont die <u>Zeitdauer</u>, bis etwas eintritt (häufig in bezug auf die <u>Zukunft</u>)
	The party isn't tonight, it's not until next week.

Erst wenn Sie sich diese Unterschiede klargemacht haben, sollten Sie das nächste Stichwort in Angriff nehmen; oder anders ausgedrückt:

Do<u>n't</u> go on to the next item <u>until</u> you've really understood this one (and done the test, of course)!

> Übersetzen Sie:
>
> **1.** Das Mittagessen wird erst um zwei fertig sein.
>
> **2.** Der Scheck ist erst vorgestern angekommen.
>
> **3.** Er wird erst nächstes Jahr fünfzig.
>
> **4.** Sie haben erst ein Spiel gewonnen.

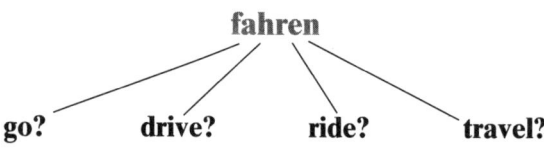

It's all go!

I hate <u>driving to work</u> every morning – even with all these car pools the traffic jams don't seem to have got any better. So I'm considering <u>going by public transport</u>. But of course you've always got to reckon with strikes, and <u>travelling all that way</u> on the crowded London underground could be quite nerve-racking, too. Perhaps I should get myself a motorbike and <u>ride</u> to work <u>on</u> that. <u>Travelling</u> to and from work is sometimes more difficult than work itself. No wonder my husband has decided to opt out of the rat race and go in for desktop publishing at home.

---

car pool – Fahrgemeinschaft ***nerve-racking*** – nervenaufreibend ***opt out*** – aussteigen ***rat race*** – Hektik des Berufsalltags

go	die geläufigste Übersetzung von „fahren", ohne die Art des Fortkommens zu nennen
	I'm going to Manchester tomorrow for a job interview.
	Mit Betonung auf das Verkehrsmittel:
	go by car/bus/train/underground/motorbike usw. (antwortet auf die Frage „wie?")
	Alternativ hierzu:
	take the car/bus/train/boat usw.
drive	**1.** (selbst) mit dem Auto usw. fahren (betont die <u>Art</u> des Transports bzw. die Fahr<u>tätigkeit</u>)
	You're not too old to learn to drive.
	2. (ein Auto usw.) steuern, lenken, fahren
	I don't know how you manage to drive that old jeep.
	3. (jd.) fahren, im Auto usw. mitnehmen
	It'll be easier if I drive you there.
ride	**1.** ([ein] Fahrrad oder Motorrad) fahren
	ride a bicycle/bike/motorbike
	2. *ride on a bus / on the underground / on a motorbike* usw.
	mit dem Bus / der U-Bahn / dem Motorrad usw. fahren (betont die <u>Art</u> der Fortbewegung bzw. das <u>Erlebnis</u>)
	I love riding on the top of double-deckers.

travel   **1.** (eine meist lange Strecke) fahren; reisen

We spent four weeks travelling through Greece.

Richard hates travelling long distances.

2. ***travel on/by*** usw. – fahren mit

She feels sick if she travels on buses, on the underground or by boat.

---

go, drive, ride oder *travel?* Setzen Sie die passende Form ein.

"Where are you _____ for your next holiday?" "Burgundy, although we can't decide how to _____ – whether to _____ by train or take the car. I don't particularly like _____, although you're more independent with the car, of course. We usually _____ long distances on the train, but I think this time Valerie would like us to have the car so that she can be _____ around from one Gothic cathedral to the next in comfort."

Fehler

mistake?   error?   fault?   flaw?

Checkmate

Secretary: *Yes, I'm afraid I made a <u>mistake</u>.*
Boss: *Made a <u>mistake</u>?! It was an absolute disaster!*
Secretary: *Well, I don't think it was my fault entirely. I am rather overworked, you know.*
Boss: *There's no excuse for it. To start with, there were at least 10 <u>typing errors</u> in the letter – or were they perhaps <u>spelling mistakes</u>? And then you put it in the wrong envelope!*
Secretary: *Well, if the letter was so terrible, you should be glad Sir Harry never got it. In fact, I actually saved the situation.*
Boss: *There seems to be some <u>flaw in your argument</u>, Jane. And I refuse to keep putting your blunders down to human error. You're fired!*
Secretary: *I think you're making a big <u>mistake</u>, Mr Dobson. You see, I'll be paying my Uncle Harry a visit this weekend – it's his 90th birthday. And if you really want that £10,000 cheque for your new project ...*

---

mistake	Fehler, Irrtum, Vergehen; die geläufigste Übersetzung
	make a mistake – einen Fehler machen/begehen *spelling mistake* – Rechtschreibfehler
	Your homework is full of mistakes again.
error	Fehler, Irrtum; etwas gehobener als *mistake* und besonders in folgenden Kombinationen:
	typing error – Tippfehler *printing error* – Druckfehler (auch *misprint*)
	Übrigens: *human error* – menschliches Versagen

fault	**1.** (technischer) Defekt, Materialfehler
	technical/electrical fault
	There seems to be a fault in the engine.
	2. Schuld, Fehler (mit Schuldzuweisung verbunden)
	It's your fault. – Du bist schuld (daran). *It's not my fault.* – Ich kann nichts dafür.
flaw	**1.** Defekt, Materialfehler, Schwachstelle (meist nicht auf Anhieb ersichtlich)
	There's a flaw in this vase.
	2. logischer Fehler/Schwachpunkt
	Whenever I make a new suggestion you find some flaw in it.
	3. Charakterfehler
	It's just one of his many character flaws.

mistake, error, fault oder *flaw?* (Try not to make any mistakes!)

If I hadn't been up all night trying to decide whether there was a _____ in the computer or the software, I wouldn't be making so many _____ (*pl.*) writing this letter. Or there's something wrong with the printer and the _____ (*pl.*) are all printing _____ (*pl.*). It's probably my own fault for buying the cheapest word processor in town. My husband says it's a character _____ of mine always insisting on buying cheap rubbish, but I can't help it if I've got Scottish ancestors, can I?

---

word processor – Textverarbeitungsgerät

fertig sein

be ready?   have finished?

Ready and waiting

Mrs Wilson: *Well, <u>I'm ready</u>. I've been standing here with my hat and coat on for at least ten minutes. <u>Have you two finished</u> with what you were doing?*

Sally: *Just a second, Mum; <u>I've nearly finished</u>. I'm just sewing a button on my blouse. It came off just as I was putting it on.*

Mr Wilson: *<u>I haven't quite finished</u>. I'm just filling in these football pools. Surely it's worth waiting five minutes for a million pounds!*

Mrs Wilson: *Honestly, <u>you two are never ready</u> on time.*

Sally: *Oh, Mum, there's no great rush. Anyway, I think <u>we're all ready to go</u> now. Let's see if we're luckier at bingo than Dad has been with the pools for the last fifteen years.*

(football) pools – (etwa) (Fußball)Toto   *bingo* – Zahlenlotto

Die arme Mrs Wilson ist wieder mal ganz fix und fertig nach all der Warterei. Hoffentlich macht Sie dieses Stichwort nicht so schnell fertig. Sind Sie bereit fürs Kästchen?

---

be ready   bereit sein, um etwas zu tun/unternehmen

I've got my case packed, so I'm ready.

Sehr oft in der Konstruktion:

be ready to do s.th.

💡 *be ready* – bereit sein

have finished   (mit etwas) fertig sein, (etwas) beendet haben

I've spent all morning feeding this data into the computer. Thank goodness I've finished for today.

Sehr oft in der Konstruktion:

have finished (doing) s.th.

Übrigens: „mit etwas fertig sein" heißt auch **be** *finished with s.th.*

---

be ready oder *have finished*? Setzen Sie die passende Form ein.

1. _____ you _____ your lunch? I want to clear the table.

2. _____ you _____ to go now? If we don't leave very soon, we'll miss the train.

3. Please hand in the forms when you _____ filling them in.

4. There are several patients in the waiting room, Dr Taylor. _____ you _____ to start surgery?

---

surgery – Sprechstunde

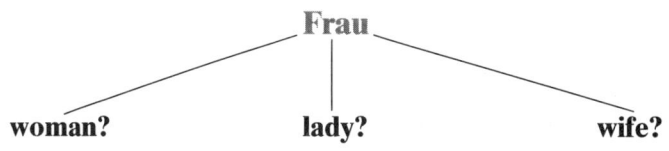

A real ladies' man

Henry the Eighth was fat, ugly, selfish and quite a hit with the <u>ladies</u>. You could say he was a classic womanizer. In fact he liked <u>women</u> so much that he had six <u>wives</u>. Unfortunately for some of them, it was a case of fatal attraction.

---

selfish – egozentrisch **womanizer** – Schürzenjäger **fatal attraction** – verhängnisvolle Anziehungskraft

---

woman	neutrale Bezeichnung für „Frau"; auch in Zusammensetzungen: *woman driver/teacher*
	Who says a woman's place is in the home?
	⚠ Pluralform *women* (Aussprache „wimin")
lady	Dame, Frau, mit Betonung auf das <u>Damenhafte</u>; <u>höfliche</u> Bezeichnung für eine Frau
	Who's that elegantly dressed lady over there?
wife	<u>Ehefrau</u>
	He got quite a shock when all three of his ex-wives turned up at the party.

Zur Erinnerung noch: *man* – Mann, *husband* – Ehemann

Und wo wir beim Thema sind:

women's lib – die Frauenemanzipation
male-female rivalries – Mann-Frau-Rivalitäten

Und noch ein Tip: Wenn Sie einen Brief an eine Frau adressieren, ist heute die moderne Form **Ms** (statt **Miss**) bzw. **Mrs** (<u>nur</u> bei <u>verheirateten</u> Frauen).

---

woman, lady oder *wife?*

I know so many _____ (*pl.*), but not one of them is good enough to be my _____. I'm looking for a really elegant _____ – someone I can show off to my friends. She doesn't have to be a very intelligent _____, but I wouldn't object if she was rich.

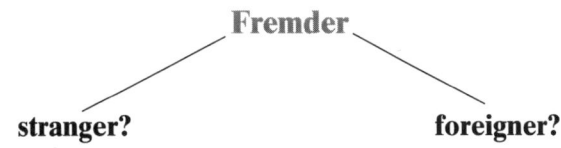

Culture shock

Sally: *I've no idea where to start looking for the shop you want, Helmut. I'm a complete <u>stranger</u> here. Although I've lived in London all my life, I've never been to Willesden before.*

Helmut: *Well, it's no good asking anyone here. They're all <u>foreigners</u>.*

Sally: *What do you mean, Helmut? You may well be the only <u>foreigner</u> around here. These people are probably all British.*

Helmut: *But everyone looks foreign.*

Sally: *You can't go by the colour of people's skin, you know. It may seem strange to you, but you'll have to get used to the idea that Britain is very much a multiracial society. I'll have to take you to the Notting Hill Carnival in August and you can see for yourself – it's just like being in the Caribbean. And you'll find the only <u>foreigners</u> there will be tourists.*

stranger	**1.** Unbekannter
	The mountain tribes are still very suspicious of strangers.
	2. *I'm a stranger here*. – Ich bin hier fremd.
	I'm a stranger here myself. This is the first time I've been to Oxford.
foreigner	Ausländer
	Foreigners can have a hard time over here. They find very few English people who speak a foreign language.
Übrigens:	„Fremden…" in Zusammensetzungen wird oft mit ***tourist*** übersetzt:
	tourist guide *tourist information centre* *the tourist industry*

---

stranger oder *foreigner?*

1. Who's that _____ over there? I've never seen him at one of Sarah's parties before.

2. You used to be able to recognize _____ (*pl.*) by the way they dressed, but fashion has become so international that it's difficult to tell which country people come from these days.

3. Mothers should keep reminding their children not to speak to _____ (*pl.*).

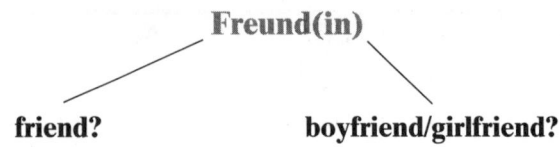

friend?   boyfriend/girlfriend?

Helmut the heartthrob

Sally's <u>a good friend of mine</u> – we've known each other for years. But she's not <u>my girlfriend</u>. The way she talks to me sometimes, though, you might think she was my wife. Sally's got a <u>boyfriend</u> already, you see. Not that I mind. I have so many girls falling for me over here, I could have a different <u>girlfriend</u> every week. But I'm not like that. Actually, I quite fancy <u>one of Sally's friends</u> – Helen's her name, I think. She has such a lovely Scottish accent. I wonder if she's doing anything tonight...

---

heartthrob – Schwarm aller Mädchen   **fall for** – sich verlieben in   **fancy** – ganz gern mögen

Ein bißchen eingebildet ist der Helmut schon, oder? Freundlicherweise hat er uns aber den Unterschied zwischen den verschiedenen Arten von Freund(in) recht anschaulich vor Augen geführt.

friend	Freund, gute(r) Bekannte(r) *He doesn't seem to have many friends.* *My friend Tom's coming to see us tomorrow.*
boyfriend	Freund, mit dem man „geht"
girlfriend	Freundin, mit der man „geht" *Are she and her boyfriend ever going to get married?*

> *friend, boyfriend* oder *girlfriend?*
>
> "Has Judith got a new _____?"
> "Yes, he's called Terry. He's a _____ from university. I can remember him – he used to spend all his time swotting in the library and wasn't at all interested in having a steady _____ then."

---

swot – pauken, büffeln   ***steady*** – fest

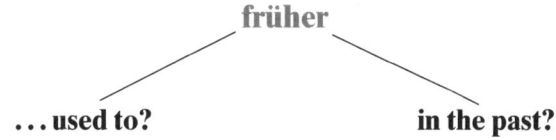

Poor Sally!

Sally: *I <u>used to go out</u> in the evenings a lot more, but these days I'm always so shattered when I get back from the office. We're definitely overworked and underpaid in our company.*

Helmut: *Well, in former times ☹ things were a lot worse.*

Sally: *In former times? You sound as if you're talking about the Middle Ages! And anyway, nobody uses that expression in everyday conversation. When we're talking about the past, we simply say <u>in the past</u>.*

Helmut: *Thank you, Sally. I was going to say that <u>in the past</u> people had a much harder time – they <u>used to work</u> far longer hours for less money.*

Sally: *Yes, I suppose we are better off these days, really. Anyway, shall we go down to the pub? I think I might just manage that. And I really fancy a drink.*

Helmut: *You know, you never <u>used to drink</u> so much, Sally.*

Sally: *It's a sign of overwork. And your bad influence.*

---

shattered – erschöpft, fertig, „kaputt"   ***we are better off*** – es geht uns schon besser
fancy – Lust haben auf

used to	die geläufigste Übersetzung von „früher" wird mit einer ***used to***-Konstruktion gebildet; dabei steht die (längst nicht mehr ausgeführte) <u>Tätigkeit</u> im Vordergrund
	I used to be a racing driver. Ich war früher Rennfahrer.
	Did you really use to smoke? Hast du früher wirklich geraucht?
in the past	wird für die weiter zurückliegende Vergangenheit verwendet (auch in Verbindung mit ***used to***); die <u>zeitliche/geschichtliche</u> Komponente steht im Vordergrund
	People managed / used to manage without cars and television in the past.
	In the past they used to put people like you in prison.

 Der Ausdruck *in former times* ist im Englischen relativ selten anzutreffen. Er ist ein gehobener Ausdruck und bedeutet im <u>historischen</u> Kontext „in der Vergangenheit" / „in früheren Zeiten".

Übersetzen Sie mit *used to* oder *in the past:*

1. Früher hatten wir drei Hunde.

2. Du warst früher nicht so lustig.

3. Früher gab es in Europa viel mehr Monarchien.

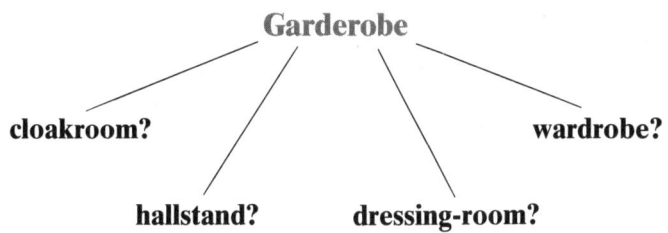

Behind the scenes

Sally: *I'd better take my coat – it's quite cold. Can you get it for me, Helmut? It's on the <u>hallstand</u>. We can leave our coats in the <u>cloakroom</u> at the theatre if we don't arrive late like the last time.*

Helmut: *Is this your coat? It looks new. You seem to have a large <u>wardrobe</u>.*

Sally: *How do you know, Helmut? You haven't seen my new bedroom yet.*

Helmut: *But I see you wearing a different outfit almost every day.*

Sally: *Oh, you mean I've got a lot of clothes! Yes, I suppose I have. You make me sound like Lady Di when you refer to my clothes as my <u>wardrobe</u>. Right then, Milord, off we go – the chauffeur will be waiting!*

Helmut: *Perhaps after the show we could go and see your cousin in her <u>dressing-room</u>. I've never been backstage before. And she does look very attractive in that photo you showed me...*

---

behind the scenes – hinter den Kulissen

cloakroom	Garderobenraum/Kleiderablage im Theater, Restaurant, Museum usw.
	After the concert we had to queue up at the cloakroom for ten minutes to get our coats.
hallstand	Garderobe als Möbelstück
	Most English homes have a hallstand in the hall.
	Übrigens: ***coat rack*** – Garderobenhaken
dressing-room	Künstlergarderobe
	Fans crowded into the star's dressing-room to congratulate her on her performance.
wardrobe	**1.** Kleiderschrank
	There's a big built-in wardrobe in the bedroom for all your clothes.
	2. (gehoben) Kleiderbestand, Garderobe
	Politicians' wives are expected to have an extensive wardrobe while their husbands seem to walk around in the same old suits.

cloakroom, hallstand oder *dressing-room?*

1. We've got so many people coming this evening, we'll have to put their coats in the spare room. There won't be enough room on the _____.

2. I really object to having to pay to leave my coat in the _____ at the Philharmonic. It ought to be free.

3. A lot of actors are quite superstitious. They always insist on having the same _____, believing it will bring them luck.

---

spare room – Gästezimmer   ***superstitious*** – abergläubisch

glücklich

happy?   **lucky?**

Don't worry, be happy

Jane: *You look very pleased with yourself.*

Clare: *Yes, I'm so <u>happy</u>. Do you remember that job I applied for? Well, there were at least sixty applicants, so I counted myself very <u>lucky</u> to be shortlisted. And then I actually got it!*

Jane: *Well, I've always said you were born under a lucky star – everything seems to fall right into your lap. Anyway, I'm very <u>happy</u> for you. Since your new job will mean a big increase in salary, I wonder if you could lend me some money?*

Clare: *You'll be lucky! I'm completely broke at the moment.*

---

applicant – Bewerber **count o.s. lucky** – sich glücklich schätzen **be shortlisted** – in die engere Wahl kommen **lucky star** – Glücksstern **lap** – Schoß **You'll be lucky!** – Keine Chance! **broke** – pleite

happy	(innerlich) glücklich
	He doesn't look very happy about his pay rise.
	Those were the happiest years of our lives.
be lucky	Glück/„Schwein" haben, sich glücklich schätzen können
	Considering she had only had four driving lessons, she was lucky to have passed her test.
Übrigens:	*lucky* heißt sehr oft „Glücks...":
	lucky star, lucky day, lucky number,
	lucky charm (= Glücksbringer)

---

happy oder *lucky?*

1. Humphrey is sixty-five next year. He's not at all _____ about having to retire, although he's _____ he can stay on till then. Others have to take early retirement when they're sixty or younger.

2. He's just made a fortune on the stock market, _____ old devil. But whether it'll make him _____ is another matter.

3. You're very _____ to have such an understanding wife.

---

take early retirement – in den Vorruhestand treten   ***stock market*** – Börse

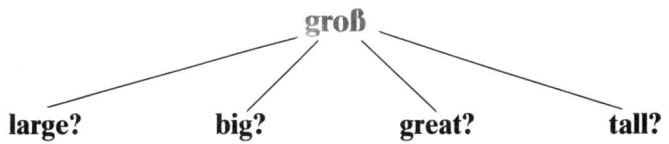

Home sweet home

Mrs Wilson: *This advertisement sounds quite interesting – DETACHED FIVE-BEDROOMED VICTORIAN HOUSE WITH <u>LARGE</u> GARDENS AT THE REAR.*

Peter: *Oh yes, I've always wanted a <u>lovely big</u> garden. It sounds great. I bet it's really expensive, though.*

Mrs Wilson: *Yes, it's only meant for the rich and <u>the great</u> with their <u>big</u> bank accounts, I'm afraid. I think we'll have to forget any <u>great</u> plans for a <u>large</u> country house surrounded by <u>tall</u> trees and acres of land ...*

Peter: *Just you wait. When I'm famous we'll have a <u>great big</u> mansion with a Rolls Royce in front of the door, and stables with race horses, and ...*

Mrs Wilson: *That's <u>big</u> talk coming from someone who may well be on the dole one day.*

---

detached – freistehend   **at the rear** – hinten   **be on the dole** – stempeln gehen

large	neutral-sachlich und etwas gehobener als *big* (vgl. hierzu auch *small* unter dem Stichwort **klein**) *This T-shirt's too small – I probably need a large size.*
big	leicht umgangssprachlich und gefühlsbetont (vgl. auch *little* unter dem Stichwort **klein**); oft steht es nach einem anderen, gefühlsbetonten Adjektiv: *a nice big hamburger, a lovely big bathroom*

great	**1.** (gehoben) sehr groß *a great crowd of people* (klingt beeindruckender als *a large crowd*) **2.** groß(artig); bezieht sich auf eine Person, die etwas Großes geleistet hat oder auf eine hervorragende Leistung usw. *a great man* ist also ein Mann mit großen Verdiensten, seine Körpergröße spielt hier keine Rolle: *Napoleon may not have been a <u>big</u> man, but for many he was a <u>great</u> statesman.* **3.** groß in Verbindung mit abstrakten Begriffen *That was a great help.*
great big	(umgs.) eine feste Fügung, in der *big* durch Voransetzung von *great* positiv oder negativ verstärkt wird *You great big idiot!* *He's drives around in a great big limousine.*
tall	groß im Sinne von hochgeschossen *a tall girl/tree/building/chimney* usw. (Hierfür kann auch *big* verwendet werden, wenn es eindeutig ist, daß es um die <u>Höhe</u> und nicht um den generellen Umfang geht.)

---

large, big, great oder *tall*?

1. The girls were so hungry after their swim that they bought themselves a great _____ bag of chips each.

2. When _____ money transfers are being handled, _____ care must be taken to enter the correct account numbers.

3. You used to have to be quite _____ to join the police force. Now height doesn't seem to matter.

Haare

hair?

What lovely hair he's got.

hairs?

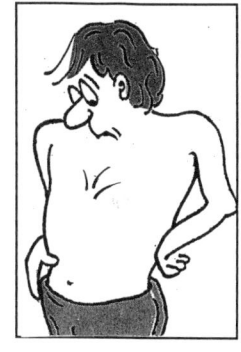

Still only five hairs?

Sie haben bestimmt nicht geahnt, mit was für einem haarigen Problem wir es hier zu tun haben. Deswegen brauchen Sie sich aber keine grauen Haare wachsen zu lassen: Es wird ja alles bis ins einzelne – doch ohne Haarspalterei – erklärt:

---

hair   die Kopfhaare als Ganzes gesehen

You've got such nice blonde hair, I don't know why you had it cut so short.

hairs   sonstige Haare am Körper (auf der Brust, im Gesicht, an den Beinen usw.), besonders wenn man sie sich einzeln vorstellt; auch einzelne Kopfhaare.

She was busy plucking some hairs from between her eyebrows.

hair kann hier benutzt werden, wenn man sich die Masse vorstellt bzw. wenn man höflich sein will:

facial hair, unwanted hair, chest hair

Have you ever tried wax to get rid of the hair on your legs?

Bei einem Satz wie *She washed her hairs*, würde man sich vorstellen, daß sie sich ihre Haare <u>einzeln</u> gewaschen hat.

---

hair oder *hairs*?

1. I wish you wouldn't comb your _____ at the table – we don't want _____ in our cornflakes.
2. I can't even remember what colour _____ he's got.
3. Did you know you're getting a few grey _____?

hören

listen (to)?   **hear?**

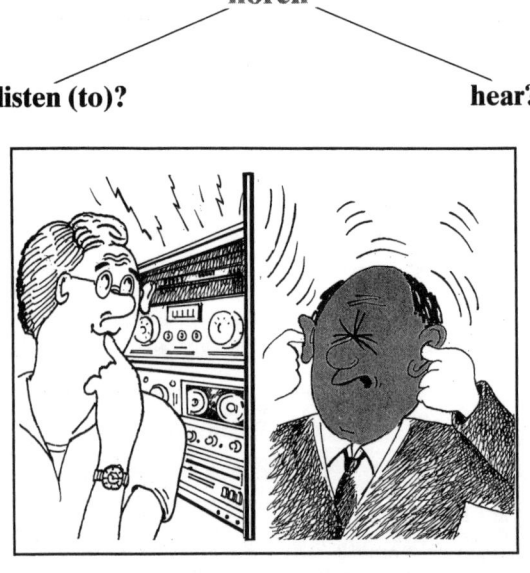

*Mr Wilson loves **listening to** Liszt's piano concertos.*

*His neighbour can **hear** the music loud and clear, too.*

listen (to)	**hear**
aufmerksam/bewußt zuhören	passiv (mit)hören
 *I love **listen**ing to **L**iszt.*	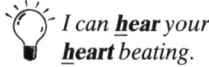 *I can **hear** your **heart** beating.*

listen (to) oder *hear*? Setzen Sie die passende Form ein.

"_____! Did you _____ that noise? It sounded like the back door. Maybe it's a burglar, or a murderer!"
"I didn't _____ a thing just now – you must be imagining things."
"Somebody was murdered in Hampstead last week, you know."
"Look, just go to sleep now, will you? I'm trying to _____ the late-night news, and I don't want to _____ another word about murderers in London."

Helmut falls head over heels

Sally: *Are you telling me you <u>met</u> this girl at the disco last night and you've decided to marry her?*

Helmut: *Yes. The moment I looked into her eyes, I knew this was the right woman for me ...*

Sally: *But don't you think you should <u>get to know</u> her a bit better first, and perhaps <u>meet</u> her parents before you take such a big step?*

Helmut: *It was love at first sight...*

Sally: *Yes, I can see that. I don't think I've ever <u>met</u> anyone who falls in love as often as you do. Anyway, I'm off to see "Kramer vs. Kramer" again; perhaps you ought to come along too – you might learn something...*

---

fall head over heels (in love) – sich über beide Ohren verlieben

Und wir wollen jetzt diese zwei Ausdrücke ein bißchen näher kennenlernen:

meet s.o.	jdm. (das erste mal) <u>begegnen</u>
	I met him at an art exhibition.
get to know s.o.	jd. über einen Zeitraum näher/besser <u>kennenlernen</u>
	It always takes me a few weeks to get to know my new pupils.

 Das kurze **meet** bezieht sich auf eine kurze Begegnung zu irgendeinem Zeit<u>punkt</u>.

Der längere Ausdruck **get to know** betont den längeren Vorgang des besseren Kennenlernens.

---

meet oder *get to know*? Setzen Sie die passende Form ein.

I first _____ Roger in prison. As we both had to do five years, we had plenty of time to _____ each other before deciding to go into business together.

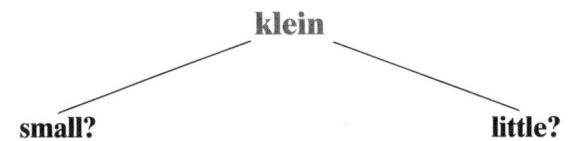

Small is beautiful

Danny: *This is a photograph of my family taken about twenty years ago – we were quite a large family, as you can see. I was the eldest of six children, and we lived in this rather <u>small</u> cottage on the edge of a <u>romantic little village</u> in Dorset. This is Julie – she's the youngest. She was <u>small</u> and fat then, and really hates this photo.*

Pauline: *Oh, but she looks a <u>sweet little girl</u>. You were lucky to have such a big family – I was an only child. I would love to have had a <u>little sister</u>. And the cottage may have been <u>small</u>, but it looks a <u>lovely little place</u>. Much nicer than the tower blocks so many large families have to live in these days.*

---

only child – Einzelkind   ***tower block*** – (großes) Hochhaus

---

small	neutral-sachlich (vgl. dazu auch *large* unter dem Stichwort **groß**)
	I would prefer the smaller TV.
little	umgangssprachlicher als *small* und gefühlsbetont (vgl. auch *big* unter dem Stichwort **groß**); oft erscheint es nach einem anderen Adjektiv, das hierdurch betont wird:
	a nasty little boy, a useful little book (*small* wäre hier falsch)
	my little sister – meine kleine (= jüngere) Schwester
	little hat auch die Funktion der Endung „-chen" im Deutschen: „ein Häuschen" – *a little house*

small oder *little*?

1. A sweet _____ old lady paid my fare on the bus when I realized I'd left my purse at home.
2. It's much cheaper to buy the large economy packs of washing powder than the _____ ones.
3. Before you sign that insurance form, you'd better have a good look at the _____ print.
4. I had lovely curly hair when I was a _____ girl.

---

economy pack – Sparpackung

What's cooking?

Peter: *Shall I cook the dinner for us tonight?*
Sally: *You cook the dinner? You can't even boil an egg properly.*
Peter: *And you sometimes make my blood boil with your sarcasm, Sally.*
Sally: *Sorry, Pete. Tell you what, why don't you make some coffee while Helmut and I get on with the serious business of making dinner? It's your favourite – rump steak with boiled potatoes and mushrooms.*
Peter: *Okay, chef, here's some strong coffee coming up...*

---

make s.o.'s blood boil – jd. zum Kochen bringen

boil	**1.**	(in Wasser, Milch usw.) kochen, im Gegensatz zu braten usw.; betont die <u>Art</u> der Zubereitung
		You boil potatoes / vegetables / rice / an egg.
	2.	kochen (Wasser, Milch usw.)
		The water's boiling – shall I put the spaghetti in?
cook	**1.**	(Gemüse, Fleisch usw.) zubereiten, kochen, im Gegensatz zu nicht kochen; die Art des Zubereitens wird nicht genannt
		How should I cook this meat / these vegetables?
	2.	(ein Gericht, das Essen) zubereiten
		When you're single, it doesn't seem worth cooking a meal every evening.
	3.	kochen; das Essen machen
		I've taught my husband to enjoy cooking.
make	**1.**	(ein Gericht, das Essen) zubereiten
		make (the) dinner – das Essen kochen
		How do you make Tandoori chicken?
	2.	(Kaffee, Tee) kochen
		Who made this tea? It's far too weak.

---

boil, cook oder *make?* Setzen Sie die passende Form ein.

1. Should we have fried rice, or should we _____ it and cut down on our calories?

2. I seem to have spent the whole day _____ tea for the workmen.

3. Who _____ for you while you were ill?

---

workmen – Handwerker

kontrollieren

check?   control?

Better late than never

My last trip to London by plane was a nightmare. We spent over an hour having our passports <u>checked</u> and luggage inspected at Passport and Customs Control. Then on the plane the steward had to <u>check</u> all our tickets as there was one passenger too many. To top it all, the pilot announced that the air-traffic controllers hadn't given permission to take off as mechanics had to <u>check</u> the instruments for a technical fault. Just as I was finding it difficult to <u>control</u> myself any longer, the pilot assured us that everything was under control and we would arrive in London with only three hours' delay.

---

to top it all – um das Maß vollzumachen   ***delay*** – Verspätung

check	(Papiere, Fahrkarten, Instrumente usw.) nachprüfen; nachsehen
	Did you remember to check the oil level?
	Denken Sie an die <u>Check</u>liste und das <u>Ein</u>checken.
control	unter Kontrolle halten/haben, steuern, regeln
	Why is it that some countries can control inflation and others can't?

Und nun, wie immer, die kleine Selbstkontrolle. Sie dürfen überprüfen, ob Sie auch alles „gecheckt" haben:

---

check oder *control*? Setzen Sie die passende Form ein.

1. After a thorough medical checkup, the doctor recommended Jim to _____ his weight regularly and try to _____ it by strict dieting.

2. House prices are skyrocketing. I wish the government would do something to _____ them.

3. All bags had to be _____ by security men before visitors were allowed into the museum.

4. The ticket inspectors are after those fare dodgers – I had my ticket _____ three times today.

---

skyrocket – in die Höhe schnellen   *fare dodger* – Schwarzfahrer

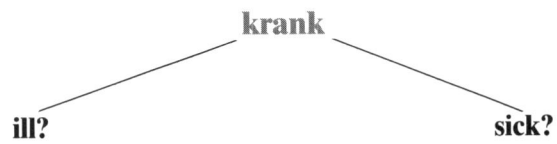

It's enough to make you sick

Helmut: *You're back early from the office, Sally. Is anything wrong?*
Sally: *It's a virus. I <u>feel</u> quite <u>ill</u>.*
Helmut: *You do <u>look ill</u>. What sort of virus is it?*
Sally: *A computer virus. It's ruined six weeks of work on our latest project.*
Helmut: *That's terrible!*
Sally: *Yes, I think I'll crawl into bed and try to forget all about it. I'll get the doctor to give me a <u>sick note</u>.*
Helmut: *It must have given you a bit of a shock – you've gone quite green.*
Sally: *Yes, in fact I think I'm going to be sick ...*
Helmut: *Hang on! I'll get you a bucket!*

ill	krank; meist mit einem Verb und fast nie vor einem Substantiv *feel ill, be ill, look ill, fall ill* *If you're so ill, you won't be able to go to Kim's party tonight either.*
sick	Beachten Sie die unterschiedlichen Bedeutungen:

1. krank, Krank(en)...; meist vor einem Substantiv

a sick child
a sick note
sick pay, sick leave

2. ***I feel sick.*** – Mir ist übel/schlecht.

I'm going to be sick. – Ich muß mich übergeben.

3. besonders Amerikanisch für *ill*

He's very sick. They're going to operate on him next week.

---

sick leave – Krankenurlaub

---

ill oder *sick?*

1. She's critically _____ and has been put into the intensive care unit.

2. I hate crossing the Channel by ferry – I always feel _____, even when the sea isn't rough.

3. One of our senior executives was suddenly taken _____ during a board meeting. He's such a workaholic, I'm not at all surprised.

4. When I smell fish frying, I always feel I want to be _____.

---

senior executive – leitender Manager   ***board meeting*** – Vorstandssitzung

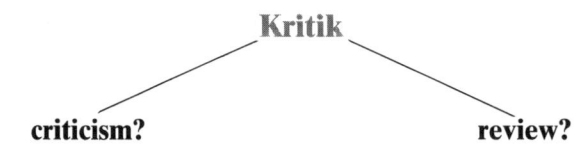

Criticising the critic

Glenda: *He can't take <u>criticism</u> from anyone – especially if you say something negative about the way he dresses. But when he writes his <u>theatre reviews</u> for the paper, he never has a good word for anyone. You'd think all his negative remarks and <u>criticisms</u> would get on the readers' nerves, not to mention the poor actors and directors who get all those bad write-ups. You should have read his devastating <u>review</u> of "Hamlet" and my performance of Ophelia!*

Lawrence: *Well, if you feel so strongly about it, perhaps you should write to the papers. But don't be too critical – you know how easily your father gets offended.*

---

director – Regisseur   *devastating* – vernichtend   *if you feel so strongly about it* – wenn es dir so sehr am Herzen liegt   *get offended* – beleidigt werden

Und jetzt wird's wieder kritisch:

criticism	**1.**	bestimmte, konkrete Kritik *That's a very fair criticism.*
	2.	das Kritisieren, Kritisiererei *All you ever hear from her is criticism.*
review		(auch ***write-up***) Rezension *Their new CD got some very good reviews.*
 ***critic***	**1.**	(auch ***reviewer***) Rezensent *He wants to be a theatre critic for one of the Sunday papers.*
	2.	Kritiker *She's a severe critic of commercial TV.*

criticism oder *review?*

"I can't stand your _____ any more. You've complained about every single one of my novels so far."
"Well, I'm only repeating what the critics say in their _____ (*pl.*)."

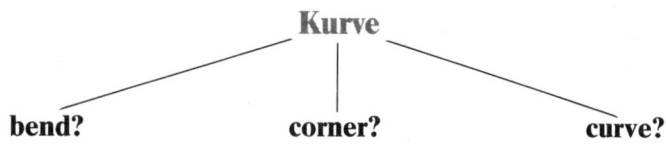

Tough going

Helmut: *Be careful, Sally! There's another one of those hairpin curves.* ☹

Sally: *You mean <u>hairpin bends</u>, Helmut; and anyway I'm used to these winding roads. You concentrate on your English and I'll worry about the driving. In geometry you can talk about a <u>curve</u>, but when we're driving we use the word <u>bend</u> or <u>corner</u>.*

Helmut: *Sally, watch out! Don't cut the bends ☹ like that!*

Sally: *Sorry, Helmut, it's <u>cut the corners</u>. I'm keeping as close to the side as I can. Anyway, the only <u>curves</u> I thought you'd be interested in are Marilyn Monroe's.*

Helmut: *Marilyn Monroe's?*

Sally: *Well, I thought she was supposed to have been the actress with the most <u>shapely curves</u> in Hollywood.*

Helmut: *Sometimes the English language just drives me round the bend!*

---

tough going – schwieriges Vorankommen   **shapely** – wohlgeformt

Ja, beim letzten Satz hat er es richtig getroffen, und recht hat er noch dazu: Die Feinheiten der englischen Sprache sind manchmal schon zum Verrücktwerden – *they drive you round the bend*. Aber ein bißchen Übung, und Helmut kriegt bestimmt noch die Kurve. Sie hoffentlich auch!

bend	Kurve einer Straße
	The bends in this road are making me feel sick.
corner	Straßenkurve in bestimmten festen Fügungen
	<u>c</u>ut the <u>c</u>orner – die Kurve schneiden
	take the corner too fast – zu schnell in die Kurve gehen
	Und im übertragenen Sinn:
	try to cut corners – den schnellen Weg suchen
	You can't cut corners learning English. – Beim Englischlernen gibt es keine bequemen Wege.
curve	**1.** geometrische/graphische Kurve; Bogen, Kurvenverlauf
	The curve on the graph showed a slight increase in sales.
	The coastline stretched away in a gentle curve.
	2. (pl., humorvoll) die körperlichen Rundungen
	She was wearing a dress that hugged her curves.

bend, corner oder *curve?*

1. Careful when you're driving – that road is full of sharp _____ (*pl.*).

2. This is supposed to be a straight line, not a _____.

3. I wish the students would keep to the footpath instead of always cutting the _____ (*pl.*).

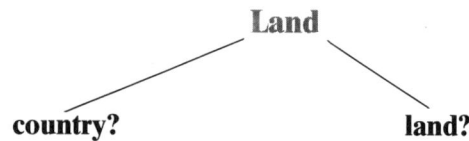

Going to the dogs

What is this <u>country</u> coming to? We used to think it was wonderful – people would call it a <u>land of plenty</u>, the <u>land of the free</u> and so on. But when you look at the dreadful economic situation, the unemployment and crime rates, and the growing gap between rich and poor, it makes you want to emigrate. Yes, I think that's what I'll do – I'll move to a sunnier climate, buy myself a little plot of <u>land</u> out in the <u>country</u> somewhere and cultivate my garden. And maybe when I'm old and grey I'll come back and visit the <u>country</u> I grew up in to see whether anything has improved ...

---

be going to the dogs – vor die Hunde gehen

country	**1.**	Land im geographischen Sinn
		The package tour was good value for money – we saw five countries in two weeks.
	2.	Land im Gegensatz zu Stadt
		life in the country – das Leben auf dem Land
land	**1.**	literarische bzw. emotionale Bezeichnung für „Land" / „Nation"; oft in einer festen Fügung
		a land of milk and honey
		He told us of faraway lands and exotic cities.
	2.	Grund(besitz)
		All this land, as far as the eye can see, belongs to me.
		plot/piece of land – Grundstück
	3.	Festland; Land im Gegensatz zum Meer
		After being on the raft for a week, the refugees finally sighted land.

---

package tour – Pauschalreise   ***good value for money*** – sehr preiswert, sein Geld wert

---

country oder *land*?

1. If you could choose, which _____ would you like to live in?

2. Japan is known as the "_____ of the Rising Sun", though some people call it the "_____ of the Rising Yen".

3. He's always boasting about how many different _____ (*pl.*) he's visited.

4. You have to be rich to buy _____ in this _____, or else marry one of the royals.

Landschaft

countryside?   **scenery?**   **landscape?**

Slow progress

Mrs Wilson: *You see so much more when you travel by train. The <u>countryside</u> around here is just beautiful.*

Mr Wilson: *Yes, we've seen some <u>lovely scenery</u>. It makes a change from the <u>bleak landscapes</u> we saw up in Iceland last summer.*

Mrs Wilson: *I've always dreamed of a holiday in Ireland, and here we are, surrounded by all this wonderful <u>green countryside</u>...*

Mr Wilson: *Yes, here we are, stuck in the middle of nowhere, not knowing whether the train's broken down or the driver's gone off to the nearest pub for a drink.*

Mrs Wilson: *As I was saying, you see a lot more of the <u>countryside</u> from a train...*

---

bleak – trostlos, trist

countryside	betont das Erlebnis der Landschaft als Ganzes und oft den anmutigen Charakter; für den Engländer heißt *countryside* vorwiegend sattes Grün, sanfte Hügel und Felder usw. *A few weeks in the Devon countryside will do you the world of good.*
scenery	Landschaft mit Betonung auf deren (beeindruckenden) Schönheit; Landschaft, wie sie an einem (z. B. beim Zugfahren) vorbeizieht *We saw so much spectacular scenery on our bicycle tour through New Zealand.*

landscape	1. Landschaftsbild, Landschaft aus der Ferne betrachtet
	From the top of that hill you get a marvellous view of the whole landscape.
	a landscape – auch „Landschaftsbild" in der Malerei
	2. neutrale, fast wissenschaftliche Bezeichnung; betont den (geologischen) Charakter, die Konturen der Landschaft, und wird oft mit flachen und/oder trostlosen Gegenden assoziiert
	The film is set in a flat, grey, windswept Siberian landscape.
	landscape architect/gardener/artist
	vgl. *moonscape* (Mondlandschaft) *townscape* (Stadtansicht) *seascape* (Meeresansicht/Seestück)

---

countryside, scenery oder *landscape?*

1. It's a volcanic _____ with very unusual vegetation.

2. I'm really looking forward to our holiday in Ireland – all that lovely _____ to go for long walks in.

3. We saw some marvellous _____ driving along the Californian coast.

lassen

let?   leave?

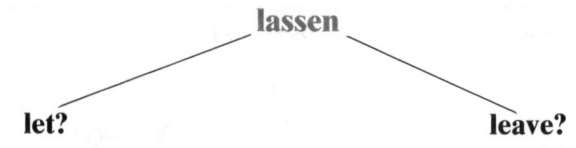

Leave it to me!

Don't forget to <u>let</u> the cat out before you go to bed, but don't <u>leave</u> him out all night. And when you <u>let</u> him in, don't <u>leave</u> the door unlocked again. We don't want to <u>let</u> the burglars in as well.

---

burglar – Einbrecher

Let the water out. (= run out) *Let him in now.* (= come in) Der Zustand wird **geändert**.	*Leave the money here.* (= where it is) *Leave him in the garden.* (= where he is) Der Zustand **bleibt unverändert**.

let oder *leave?* Setzen Sie die passende Form ein.

1. There have been so many bomb scares in Britain that people travelling are warned not to _____ their luggage unattended.
2. Being a painter, I need a flat with large windows that _____ in plenty of light.
3. Oliver was so afraid of the dark that he begged his mother to _____ the light on in the hall.
4. Most European countries are trying to control the flood of immigrants and are refusing to _____ many of them enter the country.

---

bomb scare – Bombenwarnung   ***unattended*** – unbeaufsichtigt

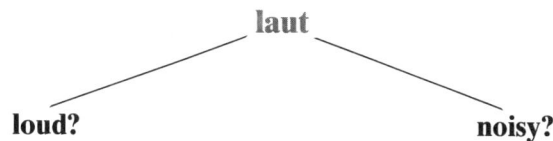

Noise pollution

Peter: *I can't hear you. What did you say?*

Mrs Wilson: *I wasn't speaking to you, I was muttering to myself. Anyway, that music's so <u>loud</u> it's impossible to hold a conversation here.*

Peter: *But it's heavy metal, Mum – it's got to be <u>loud</u>. You needn't worry about the people next door; they're very <u>noisy</u> themselves. You can often hear their <u>loud</u> voices and laughter quite late at night.*

Mrs Wilson: *Well, just because we have one lot of <u>noisy</u> neighbours, there's no need to deafen the whole street with our new stereo.*

---

noise pollution – „Lärmverschmutzung", Lärmbelästigung(en)

loud	laut vom <u>Ton</u> her (das Gegenteil wäre „leise"); beschreibt Dinge, die direkt mit einem Ton in Verbindung gesetzt werden (denken Sie an <u>Laut</u>stärke)

a loud voice/stereo/engine
loud music/laughter/clapping

Wird besonders auch für <u>kurze</u> Laute oder Geräusche verwendet:

a loud bang/scream/crash/noise

noisy	(anhaltend oder dauerhaft) lärmend, geräuschvoll (das Gegenteil wäre „ruhig"); bezieht sich eher auf die <u>Geräuschkulisse</u> und wird meist als unangenehm empfunden

a noisy place/restaurant/street/person/family/car
noisy children/traffic/aircraft

We've got very <u>n</u>oisy <u>n</u>eighbours. They stamp about like a herd of elephants.

---

loud oder *noisy?*

1. I work with ten other typists in an open-plan office. It's terribly _____.

2. The _____ music and the _____ people were getting on my nerves, so I went home.

3. Do you have to turn the radio up so _____?

---

open-plan office – Großraumbüro

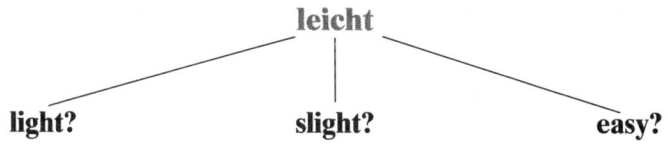

Taking things lightly

Mrs Wilson: *I've got a <u>slight headache</u> and I feel a bit shivery. I think I'm coming down with something.*

Mr Wilson: *I'm not surprised. It was quite chilly yesterday and you were only wearing a <u>light summer dress</u>.*

Mrs Wilson: *Well, it's not so <u>easy to tell</u> what the weather's going to be like at this time of year.*

Mr Wilson: *That's true. Anyway, I don't suppose it's anything serious – you'll probably just get a <u>slight cold</u>. Next time wear something more suitable.*

Mrs Wilson: *That's <u>easier said than done</u>.*

---

take s.th. lightly – etwas auf die leichte Schulter nehmen   **be coming down with s.th.** – etwas ausbrüten   **I feel shivery** – mich fröstelt   **chilly** – kühl   **suitable** – passend

Gar nicht so leicht, oder? Aber um Ihnen die Arbeit ein wenig zu erleichtern, haben wir das Kästchen möglichst leichtverdaulich gestaltet. Wohl bekommt's!

light	**1.** von geringem Gewicht
	That leather case is much too heavy for you to carry. Try this one – it's nice and light.
	2. leichtverdaulich, auch im übertragenen Sinn anspruchslos, unterhaltsam
	light music/entertainment/reading
	In summer when it's hot I prefer a light lunch.
	I usually read a magazine in the evening – I like something light before I go to bed.

slight	geringfügig, unbedeutend
	a slight headache/cold/pain/temperature/error
	There has been a slight improvement in the patient's health.
easy	einfach, mühelos
	A lot of men claim that housework has become very easy with all the modern household appliances. They should try it more often!

household appliance – Haushaltsgerät

light, slight oder *easy?*

1. Helmut's English is really very good. He's just got a _____ German accent, but you hardly notice it.

2. You don't weigh much. You're as _____ as a feather.

3. The plane had to make a forced landing, but fortunately no one was hurt and there was only _____ damage to one of the wings.

4. It's relatively _____ for young children to pick up a foreign language.

leihen

borrow?   **lend?**

Bringing up parents

Why don't you <u>borrow</u> money <u>from</u> the bank, Dad, instead of always asking me to <u>lend you</u> some? And I wish you wouldn't keep taking my comics away – I told you I'll be glad to <u>lend them to you</u> if you ask me first.

---

borrow s.th. from s.o. – sich etwas von jdm. leihen

You <u>b</u>orrow money from a <u>b</u>ank.

lend s.o. s.th., lend s.th. (out) to s.o.
– jdm. etwas <u>her</u>leihen; erscheint oft mit einem Possessivpronomen zusammen (*my, your* usw.)

I lent him my bike. / I lent my bike (out) to him.

My sister won't lend me the money.

Bei ***borrow*** bekommt man etwas,
bei ***lend*** wird man etwas l<u>o</u>s.

borrow oder *lend?* Setzen Sie die passende Form ein.

"I _____ Jenny's video recorder last night, but I've broken it. D'you think you could _____ me yours?"
"You've got a nerve. The last time I _____ something to you, I never got it back."
"What was it I _____ from you, then?"
"My boyfriend!"

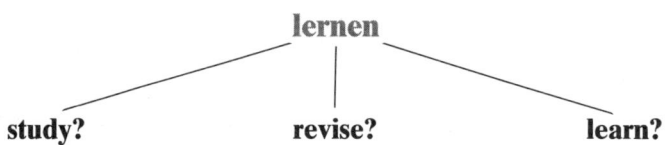

Give me a break!

Mrs Wilson: *If you've got an English exam tomorrow, Helmut, I think you'd better stay in and <u>study for it</u> instead of going out with the girls again.*

Helmut: *But I've been <u>revising</u> all week, Mrs Wilson. I've <u>learnt my tenses</u> and I've <u>revised</u> nearly all <u>my</u> old <u>vocabulary</u>. I need to relax now, otherwise I'll be too nervous to concentrate tomorrow.*

Mrs Wilson: *The last time you went out the night before an English test, you were so relaxed we couldn't get you out of bed the next morning. I sincerely hope this isn't the way you <u>study for your exams</u> at university in Germany.*

Das will gelernt sein! Deswegen geht's mit dem Studieren gleich weiter:

study	betont die Lerntätigkeit / die geistige Auseinandersetzung zum besseren Verständnis
	Why is it that the weather's always so nice when I have to stay inside and study?
	study for an exam – auf eine Prüfung lernen
revise	**1.** lernen durch <u>Wiederholung</u>
	He was up all night revising for his biology exams.
	Übrigens: ***swot (up)*** = pauken, büffeln
	2. (Stoff) wiederholen
	I've still got to revise my lecture notes.
learn	(etwas) lernen; die Beherrschung des Lernstoffs steht im Vordergrund
	learn a language *learn one's grammar/tenses/vocabulary*
	I spend so much time studying, yet I don't seem to be learning very much.

---

lecture – Vorlesung

> *study, revise* oder *learn?* Setzen Sie die passende Form ein.
>
> "You look tired – have you been locked away in your room _____ again?"
> "Yes, I've been _____ all this term's history. I had to _____ so many new dates for the test tomorrow, and _____ all the old ones. But even though I know all these dates off by heart, I don't feel I've really _____ very much about the subject."

---

term – Trimester ***know s.th. off by heart*** – etwas auswendig kennen/wissen

Fun and games

I love going out with Derek – he's <u>great fun</u>. He's got so many <u>funny jokes and stories</u> up his sleeve, he has you in fits of laughter. It can't be much <u>fun</u> for him being married to Dorothy, though. She's so serious and never seems to see the <u>funny side</u> of things. No wonder Derek's such a comedian – it's probably the only way he can stay sane.

---

have s.th. up one's sleeve – etwas auf Lager haben ***fit of laughter*** – Lachanfall
stay sane – den Verstand bewahren, „normal" bleiben

it's fun	es macht Spaß, ist sehr unterhaltsam
	It's no fun dining out with someone who's on a diet and is a teetotaller as well.
it's funny	es ist komisch/lustig, bringt einen zum Lachen
	The clown was so funny, he even made all the grown-ups laugh.

---

teetotaller – Anti-Alkoholiker

fun oder *funny*?

1. I've never been able to appreciate slapstick comedy. What's so _____ about someone slipping on a banana skin?

2. They call New York "Fun City", but it's not much _____ if you're unemployed and have to sleep on a park bench at night.

3. For kids the circus is great _____. They find everything the clowns do _____, even the silliest things.

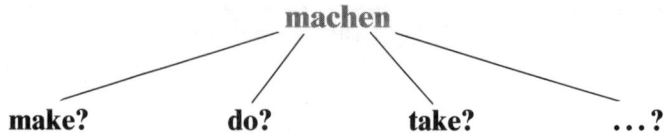

Making a mountain out of a molehill

Lucy: *I'm <u>doing</u> so much <u>overtime</u> at the moment, plus I'm <u>doing a</u> word-processing <u>course</u>, and I'm supposed to be <u>taking a test</u> next week.*

Anne: *Well, I think you <u>do</u> far too much. You're just <u>making life difficult</u> for yourself. Why don't you <u>have a break</u> and <u>take a trip</u> to the Mediterranean or somewhere?*

Lucy: *It's all right for you to <u>make suggestions</u> like that. You never seem to have any problem taking time off and <u>going on holiday</u>.*

Anne: *It's just a matter of <u>making the most of</u> life, that's all.*

---

make a mountain out of a molehill – aus einer Mücke einen Elefanten machen

Bevor wir Sie mit „machen" noch ganz fertig machen, bieten wir Ihnen lieber eine kleine Auswahl aus dem breitgefächerten Angebot an. Machen wir uns also ran an die Arbeit!

---

make   das <u>Endprodukt</u> steht im Vordergrund:

  1. etwas herstellen/produzieren

  make some tea / a cake / a mess / a noise usw.

  What are you making? – Was machst/bastelst/kochst du (da)?

  2. im Abstrakten:

  make progress – Fortschritte machen
  make a mistake – einen Fehler machen
  make a fuss – ein Theater machen

do	die Tätigkeit (das „Tun") steht im Vordergrund
	do the washing up – den Abwasch machen, abspülen ***do the/some shopping*** – Einkäufe machen ***do one's room*** – sein Zimmer machen ***do the housework*** – die Hausarbeiten machen ***do one's homework*** – seine Hausaufgaben machen ***do one's hair*** – sich die Haare machen ***do/take a course*** – einen Kurs machen ***do sports*** – Sport machen ***do overtime*** – Überstunden machen
	What are you doing? – Was machst/tust du (da)?

Feststehende Ausdrücke:

take an exam / a test – eine Prüfung machen
take a photo – ein Foto machen
take / have a break – (eine) Pause machen
take a trip to ... – eine Reise nach ... machen

go on holiday – Urlaub machen
go on a trip to ... – eine Reise nach ... machen
go on a bicycle tour – eine Radtour machen
go for a walk – einen Spaziergang machen

 have an unpleasant / a pleasant experience
eine unangenehme/angenehme Erfahrung machen

in my experience ... – ich habe die Erfahrung gemacht,
daß ...

Ergänzen Sie die fehlenden Wörter.

1. You're _____ so much noise in the kitchen – what on earth are you _____ ?

2. I just don't find any time to _____ the housework or to _____ my English homework.

3. When my husband and I _____ holiday we always like to _____ something different. Last year we _____ a bicycle tour; this year we're planning to _____ a photography course in the South of France. I've never _____ photographs before, so it should be fun.

Eating out

Helmut: *See that man over there with the funny hairstyle?*

Sally: *Which one do you <u>mean</u> exactly?*

Helmut: *The one with the silly red bow tie, sitting in the corner. Don't you <u>think</u> he looks absolutely ridiculous? I'm surprised they let him into this restaurant.*

Sally: *Just a minute, I must put my glasses on ... Hey, that's Rodney!*

Helmut: *You don't <u>mean</u> Rodney your ex-boyfriend?*

Sally: *Yes, I do. Now, Helmut, would you mind briefly explaining exactly what you <u>mean</u> by "ridiculous" before I go over and join Rod? I <u>think</u> he must be feeling a bit lonely sitting over there all by himself ...*

---

bow tie – Fliege ***ridiculous*** – lächerlich

---

think	glauben, denken
	I'm a firm believer in animal rights, but I think throwing paint at women in fur coats is going too far.
mean	**1.** (damit) sagen wollen
	What exactly do you mean by that?
	2. sich beziehen auf, sprechen von
	I mean her, the woman in the fur coat.

think oder *mean?* Setzen Sie die passende Form ein.

1. What do you _____ – shall we eat first and then go to the cinema, or eat afterwards?

2. No, I don't _____ the diamond ring, I _____ the one with the five rubies – don't you _____ it would suit me?

3. I also _____ children ought to start learning a foreign language in kindergarten.

merken

notice? **realize?**

Developing in all directions

Mrs Wilson: *Do you <u>realize</u> how much weight you're putting on?*

Mr Wilson: *No, I hadn't <u>noticed</u>, actually.*

Mrs Wilson: *Well, I can see it a mile away. I think it's time you cut down on your drinking. We don't want anyone saying you've got a beer belly, do we now?*

Mr Wilson: *Do you <u>realize</u> you're beginning to sound more and more like my mother?*

---

cut down on – einschränken   ***beer belly*** – Bierbauch

Mrs Wilson merkt aber auch alles. Und Sie haben hoffentlich den unterschiedlichen Gebrauch der zwei englischen Verben gemerkt:

notice	zufällig/nebenbei mit den Sinnen (<u>Augen</u>, <u>Ohren</u> usw.) wahrnehmen, merken
	I hadn't noticed – es war mir nicht <u>aufgefallen</u>
	Fortunately he didn't seem to notice the tomato ketchup on my tie.
realize	mit dem <u>Verstand</u> wahrnehmen, gewahr werden
	I hadn't realized – es war mir nicht <u>bewußt/klar</u>
	I didn't realize he had eaten all the salad up.
	⚠ nicht mit *recognize* verwechseln (siehe dazu auch das Stichwort **erkennen**)

---

notice oder *realize?* Setzen Sie die passende Form ein.

1. "Did you _____ how thin Jeremy looked at the wedding?" – "Yes, I did. I hardly recognized him."

2. She didn't _____ that he was just after her money.

3. I had _____ how expensive his clothes were, but I only _____ how rich he was when I happened to read that he was one of the top ten earners in the country.

---

top earner – Spitzenverdiener

It's not a load of garbage

Helmut: *What shall I do with all this <u>rubbish</u>?*

Sally: *If the dustbin's full, put it in a plastic bag. The dustmen will be emptying the bins tomorrow anyway.*

Helmut: *Dustmen?*

Sally: *Yes. Or <u>refuse collectors</u>, if you prefer their official name.*

Helmut: *But what about these bottles? We shouldn't just throw them away.*

Sally: *Well, I'm afraid the nearest bottle bank is about a mile away. I'm usually too lazy to take them there.*

Helmut: *Well I'm not. I feel very strongly about it. In Germany lots of people separate their <u>waste</u> into three different bins – one for glass, one for waste paper, and a third for general <u>household rubbish</u>.*

Sally: *Yes, I suppose it's a good idea, really. I used to think environmentalists talked a lot of rubbish, but we do seem to be producing far too much <u>waste</u> in the home.*

Helmut: *It's not just <u>household refuse</u>. Just think of all the <u>industrial waste</u> that's polluting our rivers.*

Sally: *And the lakes and seas. You're right, Helmut. We're a bit behind over here when it comes to "green awareness". I'm not surprised that some people on the Continent still call us the dirty man of Europe!*

---

bottle bank – Altglascontainer   **green awareness** – Umweltbewußtsein

rubbish	Müll, besonders Hausmüll, Abfälle
	It's amazing how much rubbish even a single-person household can produce.
	Am. und zunehmend auch Brit.: **garbage, trash**
refuse	Müll, Abfall; amtliche/formelle Bezeichnung (Betonung auf der ersten Silbe!)
	The local council is responsible for refuse collection and for providing public refuse tips.
waste	Müll mit Betonung auf die Masse; oft global gesehen und vor allem auch Industrie- und Sondermüll
	household waste, industrial waste chemical/toxic/hazardous/radioactive waste
Übrigens:	***rubbish, garbage*** und ***trash*** bedeuten salopp im übertragenen Sinn auch „Quatsch"/„Unsinn"
	Why do so many politicians talk rubbish on subjects they know nothing about?
	litter – herumliegender Abfall auf der Straße, im Park usw.

---

local council – Gemeinde   ***refuse tip*** – Müllabladeplatz

---

rubbish, refuse oder *waste?*

1. The factory was fined for pumping its _____ into a nearby river.
2. Just look at all this _____ in the streets. No wonder there are so many rats in this city.
3. Liverpool City Council has just opened three new _____ tips.

---

be fined – eine Geldstrafe zahlen müssen

nächste(r,-s)

nearest?

*Where's the **nearest** toilet?*

next?

*Where's the **next** toilet?*

---

nearest nächst**gelegen**e(r,-s), meist vom Sprecher bzw. Subjekt aus gesehen

We must get him to the nearest hospital fast.

(Es ist hier unmittelbar <u>kein</u> Krankenhaus.)

next nächste(r,-s) **in einer Reihe**, räumlich oder zeitlich

This is only the fourth floor – he works on the next floor.

I've just missed my plane to Mombasa – when's the next flight?

Noch ein Beispiel:

We took him to the <u>nearest</u> hospital, but they didn't have the necessary medical equipment, so he was rushed to the <u>next</u> hospital.

Gelegentlich, im amerikanischen Englisch sogar häufig, wird *next* in der Bedeutung von *nearest* gebraucht.

Und das nächste kleine Abenteuer:

---

nearest oder *next?*

I was crawling through the desert dying of thirst and had collapsed under an acacia tree. When a bedouin came riding along on his camel I asked him where the _____ oasis was. He told me to turn sharp right at the _____ acacia tree and carry on for two miles. When I finally got to the oasis, there was a sign up saying "Sorry, no beer". So I had a sip of water and set off for the _____ oasis, hoping to get there before the bar closed.

It's a dog's life

Man in park: *I've seen you in this park with your Rottweilers quite often. Do you live <u>nearby</u>?*

Dog owner: *No, I live on the other side of town, <u>near St John's Hospital</u>. But every time the dogs foul the paths or the grass in the <u>nearby park</u>, somebody reports me and I get fined. So we come here instead. People are much more tolerant here than in our part of town.*

Man in park: *That's what you think. I live quite <u>near here</u>, and I've been watching you and your dogs. You should be hearing from the Department of the Environment very soon...*

---

foul – verunreinigen **get/be fined** – eine Geldstrafe zahlen müssen **Department of the Environment** – Umweltministerium

near	in der Nähe von ...
	near the shops, near my school
nearby	1. in der/dessen/deren Nähe; steht oft am Satzende und bezieht sich auf einen schon genannten Ort
	We live in Richmond Road, and Dave's parents live in the council flats nearby.
	2. nahe(gelegen); steht vor einem Substantiv
	They had to tow the car to a nearby garage.
	We get a lot of noise from the nearby football stadium.

In dieser Bedeutung steht der Artikel (*a/the*) immer vor *nearby*:

a nearby hospital
the nearby airport

Ein beliebter Fehler, den Sie auf jeden Fall vermeiden sollten, ist zu sagen *nearby the* ...

Richtig heißt es: *near the* ...

Übrigens: „in der Nähe" wird auch oft übersetzt als *near there, not far away, in the vicinity/area*

---

council flats – (etwa) Sozialwohnungen   *tow* – abschleppen

---

near oder *nearby*?

George's new company is on the other side of the river, _____ the race track. We're hoping to find a suitable house _____, although I haven't seen a supermarket anywhere _____ there. The children will have to switch to the _____ comprehensive school, which I've heard is awful.

---

switch to – überwechseln auf   *comprehensive (school)* – Gesamtschule

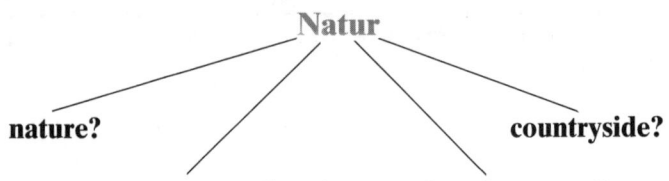

Man versus nature

I love being out in the open – the <u>countryside</u>, the mountains, the sea, I can't live without them. But when I see what our "civilized" societies are doing to our <u>natural environment</u>, it makes me quite ill. Not even intelligent people seem to understand the most basic <u>laws of nature</u>. Don't they realize we weren't put on this earth to conquer <u>nature</u> but to live in harmony with her? If people go on destroying the <u>balance of nature</u> the way they have been doing, there won't be any <u>natural surroundings</u> left for us to enjoy.

---

nature (kein Artikel!) abstrakt oder poetisch; die Schöpfung, die Naturgewalt

the forces/laws/wonders/balance of nature
mother nature, man and nature, a freak of nature

natural surroundings
natürliche <u>Umgebung</u>, konkret gesehen

Building a motorway link to the airport along here is going to spoil the natural surroundings completely.

natural environment
Umwelt, abstrakt und oft global gesehen

It's our children who will suffer for the crimes we're committing against our natural environment.

the countryside (and the sea/mountains)
Natur, Landschaft als <u>Erlebnis</u>; wird im Englischen präzisiert

He loves being in the countryside / in the mountains. / He loves the mountains and the sea. usw. –
Er liebt die Natur.

nature, natural surroundings, natural environment oder *countryside*?

1. Why don't you go to Tuscany? The _____ there is beautiful.

2. A lot more ought to be done to preserve our _____.

3. These bizarrely shaped rocks are a freak of _____.

4. The island is perfect for nature lovers and sunseekers, offering unspoilt _____ and plenty of sun.

---

preserve – erhalten   ***sunseeker*** – Sonnenanbeter

Paar

pair?   couple?

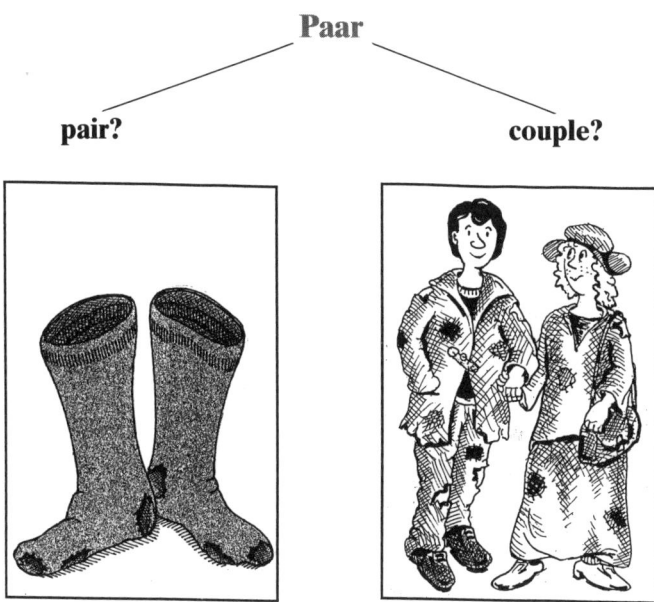

What a pair!

Helmut: *Just look at this, Sally – I bought <u>a new pair of socks</u> last week and they're already full of holes.*

Sally: *Well, a couple of days ago I got myself this expensive <u>pair of boots</u>, and one of the heels has just come off.*

Helmut: *We do make <u>a fine pair</u>, don't we? Perhaps we should go to the fancy-dress ball tonight as <u>a penniless couple</u> – the others might feel sorry for us and give us a couple of quid towards some new footwear!*

---

fancy-dress ball – Maskenball ***penniless*** – völlig verarmt ***quid*** – (umgs.) Pfund

a pair (of)	ein Paar (Socken, Schuhe usw.)
	Those look like a very sensible pair of shoes. Not quite as fashionable as the other pair, of course.
	two pair<u>s</u> of socks – zwei Paar Socken
a couple	meist Mann + Frau, ein (Ehe)Paar/Liebespaar/Pärchen
	the perfect couple – das ideale Paar
	Anna and Thomas make such a nice couple.
a pair	(besonders ironisch) ein komisches/lustiges Paar
	What a strange pair those two are.
Übrigens:	
a couple (of)	(umgs.) ein paar, einige
	There were only a couple of people at the pub yesterday lunchtime.
	Can you lend me a couple of stamps?

---

pair oder *couple*?

1. Look at those two elderly people on the bench holding hands – don't they make a sweet _____ ?

2. I seem to spend an awful lot of time with my head in the snow. Perhaps I ought to buy a _____ of those compact skis for beginners.

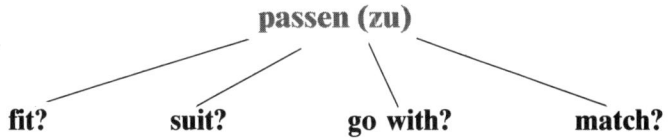

Fitting remarks?

Sally: *This dress <u>fits</u> me perfectly – it's just the right size.*
Helmut: *It is a perfect fit, but really it doesn't <u>suit</u> you at all.*
Sally: *You mean I don't look nice in it?*
Helmut: *Well, it shows too much of your legs, and anyway that shocking pink just doesn't <u>go with</u> your red hair.*
Sally: *Really? But it would <u>match</u> my new pink hat…*

---

fitting remark – passende Bemerkung   ***shocking pink*** – Pink   ***pink*** – rosa

Etwas taktvoller hätte Helmut ruhig sein können, dafür sitzen seine Bemerkungen – was das Englische angeht – ganz genau, denn bei der Mode gilt allgemein folgendes:

fit	(jdm.) in der Größe passen; gut sitzen
	This hat doesn't fit me any more.
suit s.o.	zu jdm. / jds. Typ passen, jdm. (gut) <u>stehen</u>
	I don't think shorts suit you, Grandad.
go with	(gut) passen zu, harmonisieren mit
	That green sweater goes well with the colour of your hair, but it doesn't really go with your blue trousers.
match	in Farbe/Form/Stil genau passen (zu), übereinstimmen (mit), abgestimmt sein (auf)
	I'm looking for a handbag to match these sandals.
	The shirt and jacket match perfectly.

fit, suit, go with oder *match*? Setzen Sie die passende Form ein.

Your new bikini really _____ you; it _____ your hair and _____ your new beach towel perfectly. What a pity it doesn't _____ you around the hips.

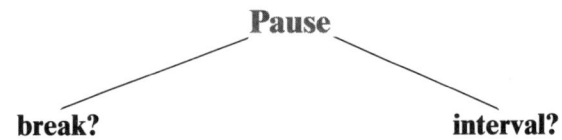

A note of discontent

First cello: *I'm dying for a drink.*

Double bass: *Yes, I could really do with a <u>break</u> too. I wish Mahler hadn't written such endlessly long symphonies.*

First cello: *Don't you hate these concerts where you have just an overture before the <u>interval</u>, and then you have to play for nearly two hours without a <u>break</u>. I don't know how I'm going to last.*

Double bass: *Well, if you're so desperate, perhaps you'd better have a drop of this. I got the barman to fill my hip flask up with brandy during the <u>interval</u>.*

First cello: *Oh, well done! Do you mind if I just hide behind your instrument for a second ...*

---

discontent – Unzufriedenheit *I could do with ...* – ich könnte ... gebrauchen *last* – es aushalten *if you're so desperate* – wenn es so dringend ist *hip flask* – Flachmann

break	Pause, durch die man eine Arbeit / eine Tätigkeit / den Unterricht usw. vorübergehend <u>unterbricht</u>, meist um auszuruhen; auch Schulpause, Mittagspause
	tea break, lunch break, morning break
	I've been revising for three hours – I think I'll have a break and make myself some tea.
	Denken Sie an *break* – Unter<u>brechung</u>
interval	vorher festgelegte Pause beim Konzert, im Theater usw.
	I don't know whether I could sit through Tannhäuser. How many intervals are there?
	Übrigens:
	• Am. und im Kino heißt es ***intermission***
	• im Sport sagt man ***half time***; *at half time* – während der Pause
pause	Zögern, kurzes Innehalten <u>beim Reden, Vortragen</u> usw.
	After a short pause to blow his nose, he carried on with his deadly boring speech.

---

break oder *interval*?

1. Unfortunately we're sitting in different rows, but I'll meet you in the foyer in the _____ .

2. I wish we had longer tea _____ (*pl.*). It would give us a chance to have a little nap.

3. Pupils are not allowed to leave the school premises during any of the _____ (*pl.*).

---

nap – Nickerchen   *premises* – Gelände

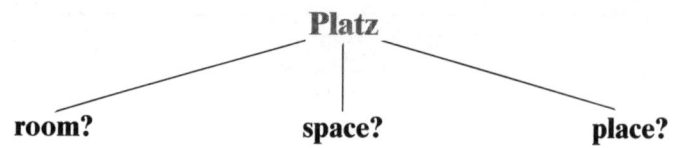

Close encounters

Helmut: *Look, there's <u>a parking space</u> over there, Sally.*

Sally: *I don't think there's enough <u>room</u> for Dad's car.*

Helmut: *There's <u>another space</u> on the other side of the square – we should fit in there.*

Sally: *Let's try that one then, but we'd better hurry otherwise there won't be any seats left at the theatre. Oh dear, I need my glasses for this. Where are they? I hope I didn't leave them lying on your seat, Helmut.*

Helmut: *Haven't I told you a hundred times to keep them <u>in one place</u>, like your handbag?*

Sally: *But there's no <u>room</u> in this handbag – it's much too small.*

Helmut: *What was that?!*

Sally: *Oh dear, I think I've bumped into the car behind us. Honestly, there really is no <u>room to move</u> in London.*

Helmut: *And it's particularly difficult to judge the <u>limited space available</u> when you're shortsighted and keep forgetting your glasses ...*

Diese letzte Bemerkung war vielleicht etwas fehl am Platze, aber die Situation – so unglücklich sie auch sein mag – zeigt uns ganz deutlich den Unterschied zwischen den verschiedenen „Plätzen". Und damit Sie in dieser Sache alle anderen vom Platz fegen können, müssen Sie sich jetzt auf die Erläuterungen voll konzentrieren.

room	verfügbarer Raum/Platz um jd./etwas herum; Bewegungsraum, Freiraum

make room – Platz machen

Well, there's plenty of room in this bed.

space	(ohne *a/an*) hier denkt man an die Abmessungen/Konturen eines Platzes

Is there enough space for this bag between the suitcases?

Wird näher bestimmt:
<u>no</u> space, <u>enough</u> space, <u>hardly any</u> space, take up <u>a lot of</u> space usw.

- Im Zweifelsfall nehmen Sie **room**, denn das stimmt fast immer.

a space	ein Platz, eine Lücke, in den/die etwas ziemlich <u>genau hineinpaßt</u>

Oh, you've left a space for the baby.

a place 1. eine ganz bestimmte Stelle, wo etwas <u>hingehört</u>

I've told you before – your place is at the foot of the bed.

2. ein Ort, eine Stelle, ein Plätzchen

This is a nice place – shall we camp here for a few nights?

Und da wir noch ein bißchen Platz haben:

seat (Sitz)Platz

I'd like a window seat, if possible.

square öffentlicher Platz (z. B. *Times Square*)

football pitch Fußballplatz

---

room, space oder *place?*

"Where on earth can I put this new exercise bike?"
"Well, there's a _____ there between the desk and your hi-fi equipment. And if you were to put all your records back into their proper _____ instead of leaving them all over the floor, you'd have plenty of _____ to do your morning exercises as well."

There's always a first time

Elderly passenger: *Excuse me, how do I fasten this seatbelt? I've never flown before.*
Businessman: *Really? This must be at least my 200th flight.*
Elderly passenger: *So you're a real globetrotter, then.*
Businessman: *Yes, but it's mostly <u>business trips</u>.*
Elderly passenger: *I'm used to travelling by train and boat, but the <u>voyage</u> to Australia to see my son and his family would have taken me weeks. It's not like going on a <u>quick boat trip</u> across the Channel.*
Businessman: *Well, at least if you had made such a <u>long journey</u> by boat, you wouldn't have to worry about jet lag. It can take you days to adjust.*
Elderly passenger: *Talking about adjusting, do you think you could loosen this seatbelt a bit? I can hardly breathe. I wouldn't like this to be my first and last <u>trip</u> to Australia.*

trip	Urlaubs- oder Geschäftsreise, auch kürzere *He's away on a business trip.* *We occasionally take weekend trips over to Wales.*
journey	betont die <u>Fahrt</u> selbst, egal, mit welchem Transportmittel; oft relativ lang oder anstrengend *The journey across the Sahara was rough but fascinating.* *How was the journey down from Liverpool?*

voyage	lange Reise mit dem Schiff (oder Raumschiff), oft mit Pionier- bzw. Abenteuercharakter (daher relativ seltener Gebrauch)

When I retire I'm going to make a long sea voyage through the Indian Ocean and the Pacific.

 Denken Sie an die Raumfähre „*Voyager*"

Aber:

- eine längere Schiffsreise heißt meistens ***cruise*** (= Kreuzfahrt)

Übrigens:

tour	Rundreise

a tour of South Africa – eine Südafrika-Rundreise

Have a good trip! – Gute Reise!

---

trip, journey oder *voyage?*

1. When I first met them they were on a honeymoon _____ to Venice.

2. I suggest that after two hours' travelling in this shaky landrover we break our _____ to stretch our legs and have something to drink.

3. We had so many dangerous and exciting experiences on our South American _____ that it was more like a 17th-century _____ of discovery.

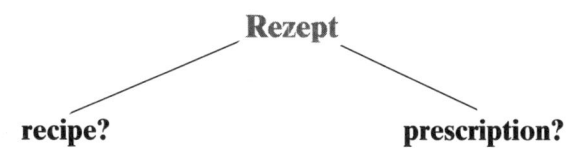

To your health!

Sally: *There's certainly something wrong with this liver of mine, Helmut. I'll really have to get hold of a new <u>recipe</u>.*

Helmut: *I'll see what I can do.*

(An hour later...)

Sally: *Where on earth have you been all this time, Helmut? You've missed your dessert, you know.*

Helmut: *I've been to the chemist's to get some medicine for that liver complaint of yours. It was quite expensive – here's the receipt.*

Sally: *My liver complaint?! I wasn't complaining about **my** liver but the liver we were eating! Anyway, how did you manage to get that medicine over the counter – I mean, without a <u>prescription</u>?*

Helmut: *A <u>prescription</u>... You mean a recipe?* ☹

Sally: *Well, what I **did** want **was** <u>a recipe to cook a new liver dish</u> and **not** <u>a prescription from the doctor</u>. My liver's perfectly all right, thank you, particularly as I hardly drink any alcohol, unlike some people I know...*

---

dessert – Nachtisch   ***unlike*** – im Gegensatz zu

Armer Helmut, er hat es wieder gut gemeint, aber leider hat er die Kalbsleber mit Sallys Leber verwechselt, weil er auf eine beliebte Wortverwechslung hereingefallen ist. Unser Rezept dagegen finden Sie im Kästchen.

recipe	Koch<u>r</u>ezept; auch Rezept im übertragenen Sinn
	Have you got a good recipe for goulash?
	Here's yet another book claiming to have the recipe for a successful marriage.
prescription	<u>ärztliches</u> Rezept
	Don't forget to fetch Grandma's prescription from the doctor's.
⚠ ***receipt***	Kassenbon, Quittung
	The receipt's in the bag.

---

recipe oder *prescription?*

1. I've forgotten how many teaspoons of curry powder to put into the sauce. I'll have to ask Gill for the _____ again.

2. You hear so many complaints about the very high _____ charges in Britain, but a lot of people – such as old-age pensioners – don't have to pay anything.

3. The young stockbroker next door seems to be a real whizz-kid – he's only 21 and he's made a fortune already. I wonder what his _____ for success is.

---

stockbroker – Börsenmakler   ***whizz-kid*** – „Senkrechtstarter"

Just sit back and relax

Sally: *You're very quiet this evening, Helmut. You haven't said a word for at least ten minutes.*

Helmut: *Ssh! I'm trying out a new learning method. You have to get into a comfortable position and sit absolutely still. After a while, when you feel completely calm and relaxed, you switch on the cassette recorder and listen to your next English lesson. And afterwards you find you remember everything.*

Sally: *It sounds like a super learning method. But what happens if you fall asleep before you switch the recorder on? ... Helmut? I said what happens... Oh well, I suppose it'll be a very quiet evening now.*

quiet	1. leise, still, keinen Lärm erzeugend; schweigsam
	be quiet, keep quiet
	You're very quiet this morning – what's up?
	2. ungestört, beschaulich
	I'm looking forward to a quiet weekend on my own.
still	bewegunglos, ruhig (Gegenteil: unruhig); meist in Fügungen wie:
	sit still, stand still usw.
	Keep still while I'm cutting your hair!
calm	gelassen, nicht aufgeregt
	stay/keep calm – die Ruhe bewahren, ruhig bleiben
	cool, calm and collected – ganz ruhig und gelassen
	The pilot managed to stay perfectly calm throughout the hijacking.

quiet, still oder *calm*?

Be _____, you lot! And sit _____, will you, until this programme's finished. How am I supposed to watch Richard Chamberlain with you children jumping up and down on the settee making animal noises? I don't know how anyone is expected to stay _____ and not lose their temper with a noisy bunch of kids like you.

---

settee – Sofa

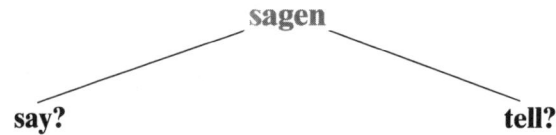

Between you and me ...

Ethel: *Do you know what Janice said?*
Hilda: *No, what did she say this time?*
Ethel: *Well, she said that Josie and Bill had a terrible row at the club last night and that Josie wants a divorce.*
Hilda: *Ethel, I've told you before not to listen to all that stupid gossip. After all, couples often argue. It doesn't mean a thing.*
Ethel: *That's what you say. But Janice told me, in confidence of course, that she saw Josie talking to Harry Evans, and everyone knows they used to be keen on each other.*
Hilda: *For heaven's sake, Ethel, I don't know how many times I've told you not to repeat what Janice says. You know she hardly ever tells the truth.*
Ethel: *Well, let's wait and see. And don't be surprised when it's my turn to say "I told you so"!*

---

row – („rau") Streit   *divorce* – Scheidung   *in confidence* – im Vertrauen   *be keen on* – „stehen auf"

say	**1.** wird benutzt, wenn keine Ergänzung mehr folgt; hier bildet es sozusagen das Schlußlicht eines Satzes

That's exactly what I said.

2. *say* + *that*

She said that she was going home.

(Hier könnte man auch das *that* fallen lassen.)

Eine Person als nachfolgende Ergänzung ist nur möglich, wenn sie mit *to* angehängt wird:

She said <u>to him</u> that she was going home.

Aber hier bevorzugt man ohnehin ***tell***, da es weniger schwerfällig klingt:

She told him (that) she was going home.

tell **1.** verlangt <u>immer</u> eine unmittelbare Ergänzung (Objekt), entweder eine Person oder etwas Abstraktes (*the truth* usw.)

I <u>told him</u> that I wasn't coming to the wedding.

She never <u>tells the truth</u>.

2. wird verwendet bei einer Aufforderung, etwas zu tun oder zu unterlassen

I <u>told her</u> not <u>to</u> smoke in bed.

Im Passiv: *<u>She</u> was told not to smoke in bed.*

---

say oder *tell*? Setzen Sie die passende Form ein.

1. Chris _____ that she often suffers from jet lag when she comes back from the States, but not the other way round.
2. She _____ him to be quiet.
3. He _____ me that he'd always been afraid of flying and _____ that he avoided travelling by plane whenever he could.

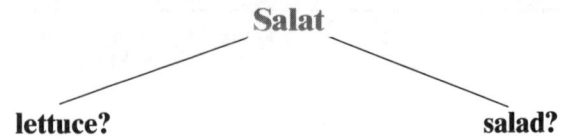

The right mix

Customer: *Waiter, I've just ordered this <u>salad</u>. I thought this was said to be a first-class vegetarian restaurant.*

Waiter: *Yes, sir – radishes, tomatoes, cucumber, <u>lettuce</u> and chives, all garden-fresh.*

Customer: *So that's how you explain the presence of these meaty slugs, is it?*

Waiter: *But there's no extra charge, sir.*

---

chives – Schnittlauch ***slug*** – (Nackt)Schnecke

Und hier noch einmal der ganze Salat:

lettuce	(<u>Kopf</u>)Salat
	We've grown some nice lettuces in the garden.
	iceberg lettuce – Eissalat
salad	<u>angemachter</u> Salat
	tomato/mixed/chicken salad
	side salad – Salat als Beilage

---

lettuce oder *salad*?

"Stop picking around in your _____ and eat it up. It's full of vitamins."
"But I hate onions, and I told you just to give me the cucumber and _____ without any onion."

Schatten

shadow?   shade?

shadow	**shade**
der <u>deutlich umrissene</u> Schatten, den ein Mensch/Gegenstand usw. <u>wirft</u>	der Schatten als <u>Schutz</u> vor der Sonne (nur im Singular)
I saw a man's shadow against the wall.	*It's 30 degrees in the shade.*

Denken Sie beim längeren *shadow* an den <u>langen</u> Schatten, den man wirft; beim kürzeren *shade* denken Sie an <u>Schutz</u>.

shadow oder *shade*?

1. You can tell it's autumn – the days are getting shorter and the _____ (*pl.*) longer.

2. If you haven't put any suntan lotion on I think you'd better go and sit in the _____, otherwise you're going to get sunburnt.

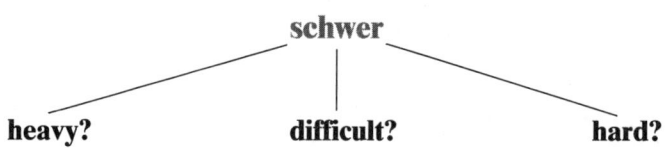

It's a hard life

Brenda: *Hello, Alec. Have you been waiting long?*
Alec: *No, I've just arrived. How are you?*
Brenda: *I'm worn out – I've had such a <u>hard</u> day. I seem to get all the really <u>heavy</u> projects at work. Do you think you could hold this for me while I look for my key?*
Alec: *Gosh, this bag's really <u>heavy</u>. What on earth have you got in it – a ton of bricks?*
Brenda: *No, just three dictionaries. The translation I'm doing is so <u>difficult</u> and I made quite a few bad mistakes in the first chapter, so I was in trouble with my boss. I've decided to do some of it at home to be on the safe side.*
Alec: *Oh, Brenda. Life's <u>hard</u> enough without ruining your evenings with work as well.*

Ja, das Leben ist schon schwer. Und wenn es Ihnen auch schwerfällt, um das Kästchen kommen wir leider nicht herum:

heavy	**1.** von großem Gewicht
	She had to drag the suitcase along the ground because it was so heavy.
	2. schwer im übertragenen Sinn; auch schwerverdaulich
	a heavy meal/wine/storm heavy reading, heavy losses
	He had a heavy cold, so he stayed off work for a few days.
difficult	schwierig, <u>kompliziert</u> (etwas gehobener als *hard*)
	I always find it so difficult to fill in my tax forms.
hard	**1.** schwierig, schwer zu vollziehen
	Is it really so hard for you to decide?
	2. anstrengend
	The place was in such a mess, it was a hard job getting it tidied up.
Übrigens:	In der Bedeutung „schwierig" sind ***difficult*** und ***hard*** oft austauschbar.

---

heavy, difficult oder *hard?*

Times are getting _____er for the police as the number of bad accidents on the motorways increases daily. Only this morning a _____ lorry crashed into a car parked on the hard shoulder. It was very _____ for the police to free the trapped passengers, several of whom had to receive emergency treatment in a nearby hospital.

---

hard shoulder – Standspur

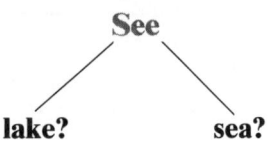

der See   **die See**

> Denken Sie beim See (*lake*) an die Regen<u>lache</u>, die ja relativ klein ist, oder an den <u>Loch</u> Ness.

lake oder *sea?*

1. Look, there's Dad on the other side of the _____.
2. The _____ air around here isn't what it used to be.
3. It only took us a few hours to drive around _____ Garda.

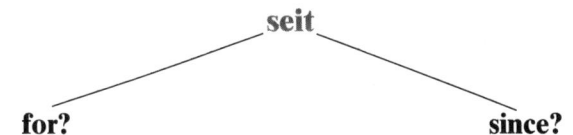

Thirsty work!

Peter: *It's only eight o'clock and Helmut's been drinking <u>for the last two hours</u> – <u>ever since the pub opened at six</u>.*

Sally: *Yes, I know. He's drunk at least four pints <u>since I arrived</u>. He claims he has to spend a lot of time in the pub to get plenty of English practice.*

Peter: *<u>For years</u> he's been complaining that English beer is flat, tasteless and lukewarm, but <u>ever since he discovered Guinness</u> he's been drinking it almost non-stop!*

---

flat – schal   **lukewarm** – lauwarm

for	**since**
Zeit**dauer**	Zeit**punkt**
Angabe der Zeitdauer meist durch eine Konstruktion mit **a/an** bzw. mit Zeitangabe im Plural (**-s**):	Genaue Angabe der Uhrzeit, des Tages usw., oder einer Handlung bzw. eines Ereignisses:
for <u>a</u> week	*since 9 o'clock*
for <u>an</u> hour	*since last Monday*
for <u>a</u> long time	*since January*
for five day<u>s</u>	*since 1963*
for hundreds of year<u>s</u>	*since he was born*
for age<u>s</u>	*since I last saw you*

for oder *since*?

Helmut has been learning English _____ a long time.

Helmut has been learning English _____ 1981.

Helmut has been learning English _____ years.

Helmut has been learning English _____ he was 14.

Helmut has drunk five pints _____ the pub opened.

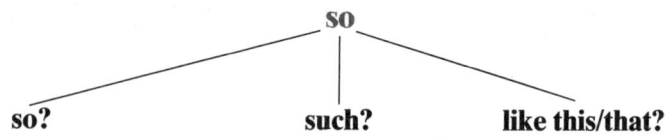

The party's over

Helmut: *Oh Sally, I'm <u>so tired</u> and there's still such a lot to clear up.*

Sally: *Well, I must say I've never seen the kitchen in <u>such an awful mess</u>, but we should have it all done by the morning. Er, Helmut, you don't put the glasses in the dish-*

washer <u>like that</u>; you have to put them in upside down – <u>like this</u>, see?

Helmut: *Sorry. I'm <u>so stupid</u> sometimes. I think you'd better do the rest before I break something. Goodnight, Sally!*

Sally: *He may be a good cook, but I've never known a man <u>like that</u> for getting out of housework!*

---

get out of – sich drücken vor

So geht's natürlich nicht. Mit **solchen** Drückebergern haben wir doch nichts gemein, oder? Da wir **so** fleißig sind, machen wir uns denn auch sofort an die Details heran:

***so* + Adjektiv/Adverb**

> *The play was so good, and all the children acted so well.*

***such* (+ a/an) (+ Adjektiv) + Substantiv** – solch

> *He's <u>such a nice</u> person.*
>
> *They're <u>such noisy</u> animals.*

Das Adjektiv kann bei Substantiven mit emotionalem Gehalt entfallen:

> *such a mess, such a fuss, such idiots*

like this, like that
vergleichend:

> **1.** solch/so (ein/eine usw.), diese <u>Art</u> von
>
> *I wish we had a car like that.*
>
> **2.** so, auf diese Weise
>
> *You don't eat it like that, you eat it like this.*

---

so, such oder *like this?*

She's _____ self-confident and thinks she knows _____ a lot. She really makes me feel _____ an idiot all the time. If it goes on _____ for much longer, I'm going to leave.

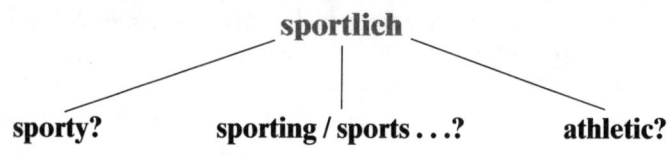

From the small ads

Eligible bachelor (26), intelligent, multilingual, good-looking, <u>athletic</u>, seeks similarly attractive, <u>sporty</u> young lady to play tennis, go skiing and share other <u>sporting activities</u> with.
Replies with photo to Helmut, Box no. XYZ 007.

---

small ads – Kleinanzeigen **eligible bachelor** – begehrter Junggeselle **box number** – Chiffre(nummer)

Und nun, für Sie, ein bißchen Denksport:

sporty	**1.**	(Person; etwas umgs.) sportlich; „sportlich sein" heißt jedoch meistens: *be keen on sport(s) / do a lot of sport(s)*
	2.	(Kleidung) salopp-sportlich, lässig; oft auch *casual* *I know you like to wear sporty clothes, but I don't think we should dress too casually for Dad's 60th birthday.*
sporting	**1.**	(Dinge, Abstraktes; auch ***sports ...***) sportlich, Sport ... *The new sports centre offers a wide range of sporting activities for young and old.*
	2.	(auch ***sportsmanlike***) im übertragenen Sinn sportlich, fair *It's very sporting of you not to charge me for the crate of whisky I dropped.*

athletic 1. (Körperbau) athletisch

I love tall, athletic men.

2. (bes. Mann) sportlich

My boys are all very athletic.

Übrigens:

sports gear/kit – Sportsachen

sportswear – Sportbekleidung

sports/sporting page – Sportteil (in der Zeitung)

⚠ *sportive* bedeutet etwa „verspielt", ist aber kein sehr geläufiges Wort

---

sporty, sporting, sports oder *athletic?*

My husband is quite an _____ person, and he's always away at some _____ event or other. I've never been a _____ type myself. I get plenty of exercise, though, with all the housework I do – especially when it comes to washing and ironing the piles of filthy sports gear Bruce regularly brings home from his rugby matches. If he was a bit more _____, he would do it himself.

Don't be such a spoilsport

Mr Travers: *I'm sorry to <u>bother you</u>, but do you think you could park your coach a bit further down the road, out of sight? It's <u>spoiling the view</u> of the valley from here.*

Mr Bradley: *Oh, sorry about that. I didn't think it would <u>bother anyone</u>.*

Mr Travers: *It's not only that. The sound of the engine when you drive off at the crack of dawn every morning <u>disturbs my sleep</u>.*

Mr Bradley: *I'm glad you mentioned it, because I just told two of my mates they could park here as well.*

Mr Travers: *Well, I'm sorry to spoil your fun, but I did buy my house here for some peace and quiet and unspoilt countryside, after all.*

---

spoilsport – Spielverderber   **coach** – Reisebus   **at the crack of dawn** – in aller Herrgottsfrühe   **mate** – Kumpel

---

bother	**1.**	(jd.) belästigen; kommt oft in Höflichkeitsfloskeln vor
		I hate to bother you, but could you lend me some milk?
	2.	(jd.) stören, irritieren, (jdm.) etwas ausmachen
		Most people complain about the noisy traffic around here, but it doesn't really bother me.
disturb	**1.**	(die Ruhe, den Schlaf, die Konzentration usw.) stören
		Can't you put those noisy birds somewhere else? They're disturbing my concentration.
	2.	(jd. bei der Arbeit, beim Schlafen usw.) stören
		Try to go up the stairs quietly so as not to disturb the baby.
		Am I disturbing you? – Störe ich (gerade)?
spoil		(die Harmonie, etwas Harmonisches) (zer)stören, beeinträchtigen, verderben
		That new office block over there completely spoils the mediaeval character of the town centre.

bother, disturb oder *spoil?* Setzen Sie die passende Form ein.

1. It doesn't really _____ me that you come home after midnight every night, but I wish you wouldn't _____ everybody by slamming the car door.

2. I hate to have to _____ you with yet another problem, but could you possibly look after my three cats this weekend?

3. I got into trouble for hanging my washing out last Sunday. The people next door complained bitterly that it was _____ their view of the back gardens.

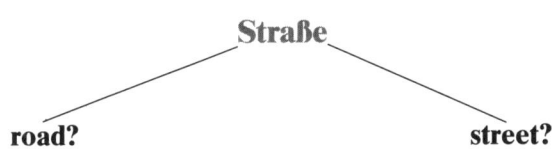

Streetwise

Mrs T.: *I wouldn't let my children play out <u>in the streets</u> on their own – there's just too much traffic <u>on the roads</u>.*
Mrs B.: *And all those <u>street people</u> with nowhere to live.*
Mrs T.: *Not to mention the <u>street gangs</u> – I'm so worried about getting mugged that I always avoid the <u>side-streets</u> at night. Even if I'm in the car I try and stick to the <u>main roads</u>.*
Mrs B.: *And then you're not safe from all those maniac drivers who think they own the <u>roads</u>.*
Mrs T.: *Yes. And isn't it funny how all the <u>roadhogs</u> seem to be men too?*

---

be streetwise – sich im harten Alltag durchschlagen können   **get mugged** – auf der Straße überfallen und beraubt werden   **roadhog** – Straßenrowdy

road	**1.** Verbindung zwischen einem Punkt A und B (außerhalb oder innerhalb einer Ortschaft); Straße <u>nach/zum/zur</u> ...
	She lived in a terraced house off the main Liverpool to Manchester road.
	Does this road go to the station?
	2. in Verbindung mit dem Fahren, dem Verkehr, der Straßenverkehrsordnung, den Straßenverhältnissen usw.; die <u>Fahrbahn</u> steht im Vordergrund
	road safety, road construction, roadworks *a road test*
street	nur <u>innerhalb</u> einer geschlossenen Ortschaft, vor allem aber in Verbindung mit dem <u>Leben</u> und dem <u>menschlichen Treiben</u> auf der Straße
	a street market, a street cleaner *street life, street fighting, street gangs* *the man in the street*
	On Saturdays the streets are swarming with people doing their weekend shopping.
	street = Straße <u>mit Bürgersteig</u>

---

terraced house – Reihenhaus   ***be swarming with*** – wimmeln von

---

road oder *street*?

1. In winter the _____ conditions in this part of Scotland can be quite bad.

2. Customs officers have seized drugs with an estimated _____ value of one million pounds.

3. It's a long way by _____. Why don't you fly?

4. They should provide some sort of community centre for all these unemployed youngsters who just hang around _____ corners all day.

---

seize – beschlagnahmen   ***community centre*** – Gemeindezentrum

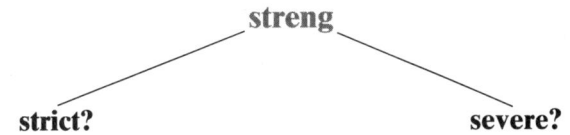

Doctor's orders

Helmut: *The doctor had rather a <u>severe expression</u> on his face when he left.*

Sally: *Yes, I know. He's very cross with Dad because he refuses to follow the <u>strict diet</u> he prescribed. It's no wonder Dad is in such terrible pain. Perhaps we ought to be a bit <u>stricter</u> when he asks for his favourite cream cakes and brandy!*

Leider sind hier die englischen Begriffe gar nicht so streng auseinanderzuhalten. Mit Hilfe einiger typischer Zusammensetzungen wollen wir Ihnen aber über den Berg helfen.

---

strict	Regeln konsequent befolgend; strenge Disziplin verlangend
	strict instructions/rules/discipline *a strict Catholic/vegetarian* *strict parents, a strict teacher* *a strict upbringing/diet*
	Und:
	strictly confidential/prohibited – streng vertraulich/verboten
severe	hart, unerbittlich
	a severe look/expression/winter *a severe sentence/punishment/judge* *severe criticism/implications*

⚠️ Verwechseln Sie das deutsche Wort „streng" nicht mit dem englischen *strong*!

a strong man   a strict teacher

---

strict oder *severe?*

In Britain the image of the _____ schoolmaster with a _____ expression on his face has disappeared. Punishments for pupils' bad behaviour have become less _____ too, and the cane has been banned. However, many people believe that the lack of _____ discipline in schools is one of the major causes of juvenile delinquency.

---

cane – Rohrstock ***juvenile deliquency*** – Jugendkriminalität

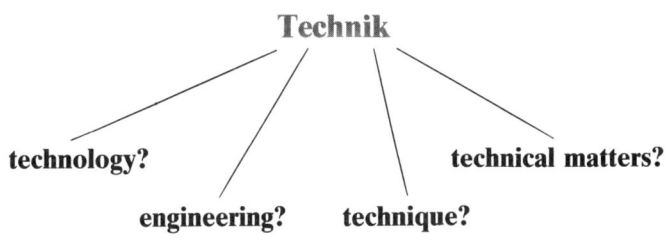

High-tech in the home

Peter: *If you ask me, all this <u>modern technology</u> in the home just makes life more complicated. I can't even get the dishwasher open, never mind get it to work.*

Mrs Wilson: *Look, there's a very <u>simple technique</u>: you turn the knob to the right, press it in, let it go again to release the lock, and the door opens – it's child's play.*

Peter: *I never was very good at <u>technical things</u>.*

Mrs Wilson: *Well, I remember not so long ago you were planning a career in <u>electrical engineering</u>. What made you change your mind?*

Peter: *All the mod cons and contraptions in this house!*

Mrs Wilson: *I've always maintained that women can cope better when it comes to <u>technical matters</u>.*

---

mod cons – moderne Gerätschaften (Abkürzung für ***modern conveniences***)
it's child's play – es ist kinderleicht   ***contraptions*** – „Apparatur"   ***maintain*** – behaupten

Tja, die Übersetzung von „Technik" scheint fast so kompliziert zu sein wie die moderne Technik selbst. Also aufgepaßt!

technology	(ohne Artikel) Technologie; die Technik im weitesten Sinn; eher der theoretische/abstrakte Begriff
	There have been some amazing developments in technology in recent decades.

engineering	(ohne Artikel)
	1. Technik in der Praxis
	The Aswan Dam is still considered to be one of the great achievements of engineering in the 20th century.
	2. zur Bezeichnung von Teilbereichen aus der Technik
	genetic engineering – Gentechnik *electrical engineering* – Elektrotechnik *civil engineering* – Hoch- und Tiefbau
technique	„Technik", Vorgehensweise, Methode, mit der etwas ausgeführt wird; bezieht sich häufig auch auf „nicht-technische" Dinge
	There's a certain technique to working Dad's video recorder.
	You must pay more attention to your technique when you practise the piano.
technical things/ matters	Technik, wobei die technischen Geräte und ihre Handhabung im Vordergrund stehen
	I haven't got a clue about technical matters.

technology, engineering, technique oder *technical matters?*

Am I really hopeless when it comes to _____, or is there some special _____ to getting this radio to work? If my husband would only take advantage of what modern _____ has to offer these days, I wouldn't have to waste my time messing around with this pre-war radio and a black-and-white TV set with only two channels. If I was the breadwinner in this house, we'd have all the latest _____ – a decent hi-fi system, a remote-control television with teletext, and an automatic washing machine and tumble-drier for Brian. Still, I suppose it's my own fault for getting married instead of finishing my electrical _____ degree.

---

breadwinner – Geldverdiener   ***remote-control ...*** – ... mit Fernbedienung
degree – Studium   ***tumble-drier*** – Wäschetrockner

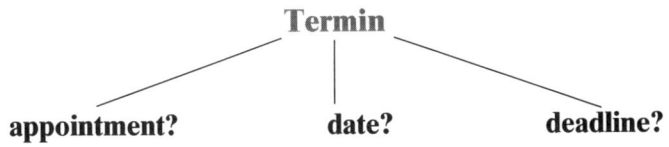

Termin

appointment?   **date?**   **deadline?**

Getting organized

Mr Wilson: *Have you seen my diary anywhere? I <u>made an appointment</u> to see the dentist and I have a feeling I should have gone yesterday.*

Sally: *Oh, Dad, you're always losing your diary and forgetting <u>appointments</u>. If I <u>fix a date</u> to see someone, I make sure I remember. If you've got so many <u>appointments to keep</u> and <u>deadlines to meet</u> you've got to get yourself organized. Why don't you buy one of those big leather diaries and glue it to your desk?*

appointment	Termin beim Arzt, beim Friseur, zum Vorstellungsgespräch usw.
	Jonathan's getting such bad marks at school, I must make an appointment with his headmaster.
date	**1.** vereinbarter/festgelegter Tag einer Verabredung, Sitzung, Lieferung usw.
	Can we fix a time and date for the next meeting?
	2. Rendezvous, Verabredung
	I've finally got a date with Mark – he's asked me out to dinner on Friday!
deadline	Fristablauf; Termin als letzte Möglichkeit, etwas einzureichen / zu erledigen usw.
	I'd better get a move on – next week is the deadline for handing in my application.

---

get a move on – „sich sputen"   ***application*** – Bewerbung, Antrag *appointment, date* oder *deadline?*

1. The writer was under tremendous pressure from her publisher – the _____ for handing in the manuscript of her latest novel was only a month away.

2. The manager has been taken seriously ill. His secretary is having to cancel all his _____ (*pl.*).

3. I'm afraid the meeting will have to be postponed to a later _____ .

---

publisher – Verleger, Verlag ***cancel*** – absagen ***postpone*** – aufschieben

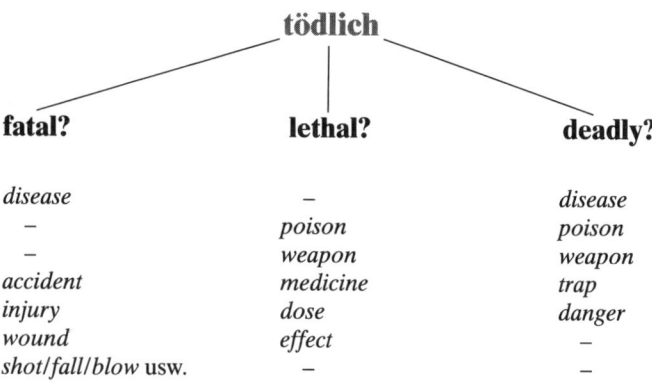

tödlich

fatal?	**lethal?**	**deadly?**
disease	–	*disease*
–	*poison*	*poison*
–	*weapon*	*weapon*
accident	*medicine*	*trap*
injury	*dose*	*danger*
wound	*effect*	–
shot/fall/blow usw.	–	–

Dead and gone

We thought he must have died in a <u>fatal accident</u> or of some <u>deadly</u> exotic <u>disease</u>. In fact he was found to have been dealing in the export of <u>lethal weapons</u> to the Middle East. Realizing he was now in mortal danger, he had decided to take his own life by injecting a <u>lethal dose</u> of morphine.

Verzeihen Sie das „tödliche" Thema, aber das Wort hat es in sich. Wir können Ihnen zwar keine todsicheren Tips geben, dafür aber einige lebenswichtige Hinweise, die Sie vor fatalen Fehlern bewahren sollen.

fatal	mit tödlichem Ausgang *The foreign minister suffered fatal injuries in the bomb attack.*
lethal	potentiell tödlich; klingt sachlicher als *deadly* *If taken in high doses, this medicine can have a lethal effect.*
deadly	**1.** potentiell tödlich; klingt dramatisch/bedrohlich *That new bread knife you bought looks like a deadly weapon!* **2.** (im übertragenen Sinn, umgs.) tödlich, unerträglich *It was such a deadly party, I nearly fell asleep.* • Oft auch vor einem Adjektiv: *deadly boring* – todlangweilig
Übrigens:	***mortal*** klingt literarisch/dramatisch und erscheint in folgenden Kombinationen: *mortal danger/wound/combat*

---

fatal, lethal oder *deadly?*

1. This cabinet contains various _____ poisons, so keep it locked at all times.

2. Three of the people involved in yesterday's pile-up on the M1 suffered _____ injuries.

3. The guerrilla troops walked straight into the _____ trap.

---

pile-up – Massenkarambolage   *M1* – Autobahn von London in Richtung Norden

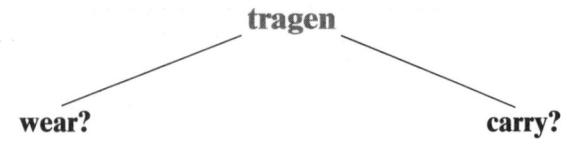

What a carry-on!

If there's one thing I can't stand it's having to <u>carry</u> a handbag. Why can't the fashion designers produce practical clothes for women to <u>wear</u> as well? I mean clothes with pockets big enough to <u>carry</u> all your bits and pieces in – such as your sunglasses, which you end up <u>wearing</u> all day and night because you can't fit them into your wretched handbag anyway.

What a carry-on! – So ein Palaver!   ***wretched*** – verflucht

wear	(Kleidung, Schmuck, Brille usw.) anhaben, aufhaben, umhaben
	I hope Grandma doesn't turn up at my 21st birthday party wearing her new jeans.
carry	tragen (in der Hand, auf dem Rücken, in der Tasche/Handtasche usw.); dabeihaben
	The women carry their babies on their backs while they work.
	I always carry my allergy ID on me.

ID – Ausweis

---

wear oder *carry*? Setzen Sie die passende Form ein.

1. Why is it that visitors to London still expect the average businessman in the City to _____ a bowler hat and _____ an umbrella?

2. Is that his real hair, or is he _____ a wig?

3. With that heavy bride's dress and all the jewellery you're planning to _____, I don't know whether I'm going to be able to _____ you over the threshold.

---

threshold – Türschwelle

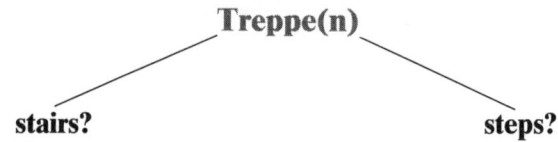

A step in the right direction

I find it so hard climbing <u>stairs</u>, not to mention having to carry heavy shopping up to my flat on the fourth floor. Why can't they put us old folks in proper houses? I could just about manage the <u>steps</u> leading up to the front door. Perhaps I should go to Dr Martin's phobia classes after all – she might be able to cure me of my fear of lifts. It's a pity her surgery's on the 12th floor ...

floor – Etage, Stock(werk)   *surgery* – Praxis

stairs	Treppe(n) im Haus oder Wohnblock
	The carpet on these stairs is so slippery – I'm surprised nobody's fallen down them yet.
steps	Treppe(n) aus <u>Stein</u>, folglich oft draußen
	When I came home I found my husband sitting on the front steps. He had locked himself out.
Übrigens:	
flight (of stairs)	Treppe, Etage, Stockwerk
	Mr Davies lives two flights further up.

stairs oder *steps*?

1. Do you have to slide down the _____ on your backside? You'll ruin your new pyjamas.
2. The _____ leading up to the castle are steep and slippery.
3. If he's in a wheelchair, it's no good putting him in a house with two flights of _____.

Übung

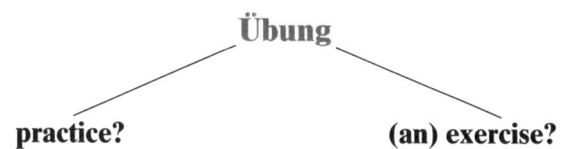

practice?   **(an) exercise?**

A little bit every day

Helmut: *I've got my English test coming up very soon and I feel my grammar's a bit rusty. I'm just out of practice.*

Sally: *There's not much wrong with your grammar as far as I can see. But if you want, we can do some exercises from your grammar book together. I'm sure half an hour's practice a day would be more than enough.*

Helmut: *Do you think I'll be able to brush it up in time for the test?*

Sally: *I'm sure you will. Remember, practice makes perfect!*

---

rusty – eingerostet   ***brush up*** – auffrischen

practice	das Üben; regelmäßige Wiederholung zum Zweck des Lernens / der Verbesserung
	Learning to ski well is just a matter of practice.
	practice makes perfect (Übung macht den Meister!)
an exercise	eine <u>einzelne</u> Übung (geistige/sportliche/ sprachliche usw.) ; eine Aufgabe
	This is a good exercise on future tenses.
	Be careful not to strain your back when you're doing your keep-fit exercises.
 **exercise**	(ohne *an*!) = körperliche Bewegung
	Too many people sit in an office all day long and don't get any exercise at all.

Und jetzt, wie üblich, eine kleine Übung:

> *practice* oder *exercise?*
>
> **1.** The neighbours were driven mad by the girl next door doing her _____ (*pl.*) on the violin.
>
> **2.** If you want to speak Russian fluently, you'll need a lot of _____.
>
> **3.** For homework will you please do the _____ on page five.

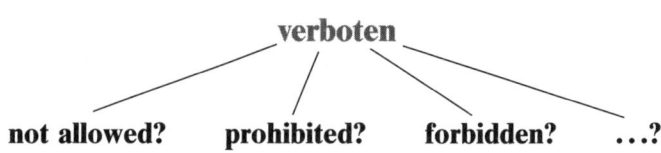

We wish you a pleasant flight

Air hostess: *Do you think you could sit up properly and fasten your seatbelt, please? <u>You're not allowed to</u> be lying down during the landing approach. And there's <u>no smoking</u> in this section of the plane.*

Passenger: *Er, could I just go to the toilet?*

Air hostess: *If you're quick. And remember – <u>smoking</u> in the lavatories and aisles <u>is absolutely forbidden</u>.*

Passenger: *I also wanted to take a picture of the pilot before we land.*

Air hostess: *Sorry, <u>no photographs</u> in the cockpit.*

Passenger: *Well, I think I'll just quietly listen to my little radio over the earphones, if that's all right.*

Air hostess: *I'm afraid radios are <u>strictly prohibited</u>, but you can listen to the music provided as part of our in-flight entertainment service.*

Passenger: *Are you absolutely sure? After all, I wouldn't like to do anything on this plane that's <u>not allowed</u>...*

---

aisle – Gang   *shot* – Schuß, Foto   *in-flight entertainment* – Bordunterhaltung

Folgende Ausführungen sehen zugegebenermaßen ziemlich verboten aus. Aber, Kästchen-Überspringen ist streng verboten!

---

you're not allowed to ...
... is/are not allowed

Die häufigsten Übersetzungen von „es ist verboten zu .../... ist verboten":

You're not allowed to wear shorts in this restaurant. / Shorts are not allowed in this restaurant.

(Auf keinen Fall: *It is not allowed to ...* ☹ !)

no smoking, no spitting, no rollerskating
no skateboards, no photographs, no entry

„... verboten!"

it is prohibited to ...
... is/are prohibited

„es ist (strengstens) verboten/untersagt zu.../...ist/sind (strengstens) verboten/untersagt"

smoking prohibited – „Rauchen verboten!"

klingt gehoben bzw. offiziell

it is forbidden to ...
... is/are forbidden

klingt bedrohlicher bzw. ist schriftsprachlich/gehoben; oft mit moralisch-religiösem Beigeschmack

In this part of the country it's forbidden for women to show their hair in public.

---

not allowed, prohibited oder *forbidden?*

1. Smoking _____. Penalty £50.

2. Children are _____ to play in the courtyard.

3. Why should women still have to suffer because Adam was tempted by the _____ fruit thousands of years ago?

während

while?   during?

Did you have a nice trip?

It was a disaster from beginning to end. <u>While I was boarding</u> the plane my straw hat flew off and landed in a pool of oil on the tarmac. <u>During the flight</u> one of the air hostesses spilt a whole tray of sticky orange juice all over me. Then <u>while I was going through customs</u> at the other end, my case burst open and everything fell out. But don't imagine that was all: <u>during the two weeks</u> I was there it snowed non-stop. That's definitely the last time I'm going to Leningrad <u>during the Easter holidays</u>.

---

tarmac – Rollfeld   **tray** – Tablett   **sticky** – klebrig

---

> ***while* + <u>Verb</u>**
>
>   *while they were watching TV, while I was asleep*
>
> ***during* + <u>Substantiv</u>**, das einen meist festumrissenen Zeitabschnitt beinhaltet
>
>   *during the lesson/exam/programme/strike*
>
> 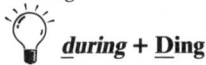 ***during* + <u>D</u>ing**
>
> Das deutsche „während" + Substantiv wird im Englischen oft durch eine <u>Verbal</u>konstruktion wiedergegeben:
>
> *while he was away* – während seiner Abwesenheit
>
> *while we were having dinner* – während des Abendessens
>
> *while I was at university* – während meines Studiums
>
> Formeller wären hier: *during his absence, during the meal, during my time at university*

while oder *during?*

1. Do you children have to jump around and make noises like chimpanzees _____ I'm trying to teach you the theory of evolution? Can't you do it _____ the lunch break?

2. _____ the ambulance strike, people had to be taken to hospital in taxis.

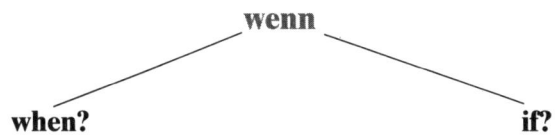

If or when...

Helmut: *When I pass my final English test, I'm going to take you all out for a slap-up meal.*

Sally: *You're very sure of yourself, Helmut. Don't you mean if you pass?*

Helmut: *Well, Sally, you've always been so good at pointing out my mistakes that I feel quite confident about my English now. Of course I'm not perfect, but I know you'll correct me if I make any more mistakes.*

Sally: *You mean when you make your next mistake...*

---

slap-up meal – tolles Essen **confident** – selbstsicher

Wenn das Wörtchen „wenn" nicht wär', wär' das Leben halb so schwer ...

when	zeitlich; es <u>steht fest</u>, <u>daß</u> etwas geschehen wird
	When I buy the computer I'll be broke.
	Die Entscheidung ist schon getroffen: nach dem Kauf wird der Käufer pleite sein.
	<u>when</u> antwortet auf die Frage „<u>wann</u>?"
if	es ist noch offen, <u>ob</u> etwas passieren wird
	If I buy the computer I'll be broke.
	Es ist nicht sicher, ob der Computer gekauft wird; nur <u>falls</u> dies geschieht, wird der Käufer pleite sein.
	i<u>f</u> = <u>f</u>alls

---

when oder *if?*

1. _____ you've got any time on Saturday, perhaps you could come round and show me how my computer works.

2. Later on, _____ you've finished in the garden, you can start peeling the potatoes.

3. _____ I ever learn to speak English properly, I'm going to emigrate to Australia.

It's all getting a bit much

Kevin: *Have you <u>gone</u> completely <u>mad</u>? Who's supposed to eat all this food? It'll <u>go bad</u> in this muggy weather.*
Rosi: *Did you say something, Kev?*
Kevin: *I think you must be <u>going deaf</u> as well. I said, all this food you bought will <u>go off</u> in the hot weather!*
Rosi: *There's no need to <u>get</u> so <u>cross</u>. I just <u>got sick and tired</u> of coming home to an empty fridge every evening.*
Kevin: *But I thought you were the one who was worried about <u>getting fat</u>. And so you should be.*
Rosi: *I'm not so much worried about putting on weight any more as <u>going grey</u> with your non-stop nagging...*

---

muggy – schwül (auch *close*, *sticky*)   *nag* – herumnörgeln, -mäkeln

Bei „werden" wird es jetzt leider etwas länger werden. Damit es aber nicht zu viel wird, beschränken wir uns auf einige repräsentative Übersetzungen.

go deaf	taub werden	*go sour*	sauer werden
go blind	blind werden	*go bad/off*	schlecht werden
go bald	kahl werden	*go pale*	blaß werden
go grey	grau werden	*go white*	weiß werden
go mad	verrückt werden	*go red*	rot werden

⚠ Bei *go* liegt die Betonung eher auf dem Endzustand, der sich oft drastisch vom Ausgangszustand unterscheidet.

In manchen Fällen kann man *go* durch das etwas gehobenere *turn* ersetzen: *turn sour/pale/grey/white/cold.*

get dark	dunkel werden	***get sick***	krank werden
get cold	kalt werden	***get tired***	müde werden
get warm/hot	warm werden	***get weak***	schwach werden
get wet	naß werden	***get old***	alt werden
get fat	dick werden	***get/fall ill***	krank werden
get rich	reich werden	***get worse***	schlimmer werden
		get better	besser werden

get cross/angry/mad wütend werden
get sick and tired of s.th. etwas satt werden

⚠ Bei ***get*** liegt die Betonung auf dem (allmählichen) Veränderungsprozeß.

Alternativ zu ***get*** gelegentlich auch das gehobenere ***grow*** (***old/weak/dark***) bzw. ***become*** (***rich/ill***).

---

go oder *get*? Setzen Sie die passende Form ein.

1. My eyesight seems to have _____ worse since I've been working in front of a computer screen.

2. When I told him, he _____ pale and then very red. Then, as the truth began to sink in, he gradually _____ angry.

3. There must be some way of _____ rich quick and enjoying life before we _____ too old and sick to do so.

4. Why do you have to keep on reminding me that I'm _____ bald and _____ fat?

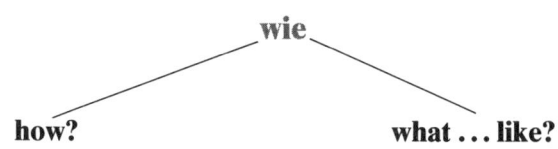

| how? | what ... like? |

| – **How** is Helmut? | – **What**'s Helmut **like**? |
| – I'm afraid he's not very well. | – He's too much of a flirt for my liking. |

Bei Personen:

| *How is Helmut?* | *What's Helmut like?* |
| (Wie <u>geht es</u> Helmut?) | (Wie <u>ist</u> Helmut so? / Was ist Helmut für ein Typ?) |

how? fragt nach der Gesundheit, dem Wohlbefinden.

what ... like? fragt nach dem Wesen/Typ, der Persönlichkeit.

Sonst:

I hear you were in Chicago. How was it?

I've never been to Chicago. What's it like?

(Wie <u>war</u> der Aufenthalt <u>für dich persönlich</u>?)

(Wie <u>ist</u> die Stadt eigentlich so?)

how? fragt nach einem persönlichen, subjektiven Erlebnis.

what ... like? fragt nach allgemeinen, „objektiven" Tatsachen.

Bei Dingen oder Ereignissen sind oft beide Alternativen möglich, je nachdem, ob die Betonung auf dem persönlichen Erlebnis (*how?*) oder auf der objektiven Beurteilung (*what ... like?*) liegt:

How was the film? (Wie hat dir der Film gefallen?)

What was the film like? (Wie war der Film?)

Auf jeden Fall sollten Sie sich folgendes merken:

 Bei Personen: ***how*** für ***health*** (= Gesundheit)

Bilden Sie Fragen: *how?* oder *what ... like?*

1. – .... ?
   (your new cleaning lady)
   – She's very good.

2. – .... ?
   (Simon)
   – Oh, he's feeling much better, thanks.

3. – .... ?
   (Andrew's school report)
   – It wasn't too bad this time.

4. – .... ?
   (you)
   – I'm fine, thanks. And you?

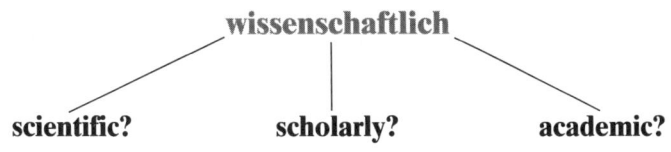

Not everybody's cup of tea

You call that a <u>scholarly piece of work</u>, do you? I call it a mess. And you say you want to go in for a university career and devote yourself to <u>academic research</u>. Well, you'll have to develop a more <u>scholarly approach</u> than this, I'm afraid. At least you're not planning on being a scientist. I can just see you blowing up a chemistry lab with some <u>scientific experiment</u>. If you really want my advice, stick to weight-lifting.

---

not everybody's cup of tea – nicht jedermanns Sache   ***devote o.s. to s.th.*** – sich einer Sache widmen   ***research*** – Forschung   ***approach*** – Einstellung   ***blow up*** – in die Luft jagen

Allzu wissenschaftlich wollen wir es hier nicht treiben, sondern Ihnen einfach ein paar Tips geben, damit Sie mit diesem wirklich verzwickten Wortfeld besser zurechtkommen:

scientific	**1.** <u>natur</u>wissenschaftlich	
	It gets more and more difficult to keep up with scientific developments these days.	
	2. wissenschaftlich <u>genau</u> / hieb- und stichfest	
	Is there any scientific proof of a link between ozone levels and asthma attacks?	
scholarly	<u>gelehrt</u>-wissenschaftlich; betont <u>positiv</u> die <u>Methode</u> einer Arbeit, des Denkens usw.	
	She has a very scholarly mind. I think she'll probably go into research of some sort.	

academic	wissenschaftlich/geistig/intellektuell/akademisch, besonders in Zusammenhang mit der Universität und mit Publikationen
	an academic career/discussion/institution/publisher/library *academic publications, the academic world*
	Why do so many academics have to write in such a highly academic style that nobody can understand what they're talking about?

Übrigens:

science	(ohne Artikel) die Wissenschaft; die Naturwissenschaft(en)
the (natural) sciences	die Naturwissenschaften
arts and sciences	Geistes- und Naturwissenschaften
the arts, the humanities	die Geisteswissenschaften
research	die Forschung, die Wissenschaft
researcher	Forscher, Wissenschaftler

scientific, scholarly oder *academic*?

1. He's thinking of an _____ career – a job at university or some other institute of higher education.

2. Lack of funds for _____ experiment and research is driving Britain's top physicists to other countries in a massive brain drain.

3. One of our main aims is to develop a _____ and balanced way of thinking among our students.

---

brain drain – Abwanderung von Wissenschaftlern/Experten

Give me a desert island

I enjoy watching football matches, but the rough behaviour of so many of the <u>spectators</u> always frightens me. Going to the cinema just gets on my nerves – those people in the <u>audience</u> who eat their popcorn noisily, repeat all the jokes, and constantly get up to fetch more snacks and drinks – the way I imagine <u>TV viewers</u> to behave within their own four walls. At least at the theatre the <u>audience</u> has to sit still until the interval, though there are always those annoying people who cough loudest or rustle their sweet papers during the most dramatic parts. Well, I must be off to that demonstration at the town hall. Why on earth did I have to choose crowd psychology as my research topic?

---

desert island – einsame Insel   **rustle** – rascheln mit   **sweet paper** – Bonbonpapier
town hall – Rathaus   **crowd psychology** – Massenpsychologie   **research topic** – Forschungsthema

spectators	(auch **crowd**) Zuschauer bei einer Sportveranstaltung *spectator sport* – Zuschauersport *There weren't many spectators / There wasn't much of a crowd at the match on Saturday.*
audience	**1.** Publikum/Zuschauer im Theater *somebody in / a member of the audience* – ein(er der) Zuschauer *Somebody in the audience was snoring during the third act.*

2. Publikum im Kino

somebody in the audience – ein Zuschauer
people in the audience – (einige) Zuschauer

viewer (Fernseh)Zuschauer; im Plural auch **audience**

The number of viewers at peak hours on Thursday nights has dropped drastically since the soap opera finished.

---

peak hours – Spitzenzeiten *soap opera* – „Seifenoper", meist niveaulose Unterhaltungsserie

---

spectators, audience oder *viewers?*

1. "How many _____ were there at the Cup final?" – "Oh, there must have been a crowd of about 100,000."

2. If enough _____ refused to pay their licence fee, the standard of TV programmes might improve.

3. How did the _____ react to that horrible scene at the beginning of the play?

Cup final – Pokalfinale *licence fee* – Fernsehgebühren

Britisch versus amerikanisch

English as a world language?

Mr Wilson's aunt, who has lived in California for forty years, is spending a few weeks in London with her relatives. One place she wasn't planning on visiting is the police station ...

Police Officer: *So you've lost your purse, Madam. Have you any idea where you might have lost it?*
Aunt Lizzie: *Well, I'd just been to the movies at Piccadilly, and then I went to a drugstore to get ...*

Police Officer: *A drugstore?*
Aunt Lizzie: *Yes, I needed something to clear my head after two hours in the <u>movie theater</u>. I wonder if I dropped my <u>purse</u> on the <u>sidewalk</u> as I was coming out of the <u>store</u> ... You see, I noticed it was gone when I was standing in the bus <u>line</u>.*
Police Officer: *Could you tell me what was in the purse?*
Aunt Lizzie: *There was my <u>driver's license</u>, some <u>cookies</u> for when I get hungry, a book for the <u>subway</u> ...*
Police Officer: *The subway?*
Aunt Lizzie: *Yes, it's one of the few chances I get to read. Then there was my <u>wallet</u>, of course, with about £50 in cash and my credit cards ...*
Police Officer: *Your wallet?*
Aunt Lizzie: *<u>Sure</u>. Where else would I keep it? And a small <u>package</u> I was going to <u>mail</u> to my husband in Santa Barbara – he just loves English <u>candies</u>.*
Police Officer: *Well, I know everything's supposed to be bigger and better in the United States, but that really takes the biscuit.*
Aunt Lizzie: *Biscuit?*

---

that takes the biscuit – das schlägt ja alles (die Amerikaner sagen für „Keks" *cookie* statt *biscuit*)

Es wird Ihnen vielleicht aufgefallen sein, daß die unterstrichenen Wörter amerikanische Ausdrücke sind, die den armen Londoner Polizeibeamten zum Teil ganz verwirrt haben. Zum Beispiel heißt *purse* im britischen Englisch „Portemonnaie", während es im Amerikanischen eine Handtasche bezeichnet, und die fallen ja etwas größer aus als der übliche Geldbeutel ...

Die anderen Mißverständnisse werden Ihnen anhand der nachstehenden Liste klar werden, die einige der geläufigeren Unterschiede im britischen und amerikanischen Wortschatz aufführt. Ausdrücke aus dem Dialog sind durch halbfette Schrift gekennzeichnet. Die mit einem Sternchen (*) gekennzeichneten „Amerikanismen" beginnen auch in Großbritannien allmählich Fuß zu fassen – ein Zeichen dafür, daß durch die heutige weltweite Kommunikation immer mehr amerikanisches Wortgut seinen Weg über den Atlantik findet.

britisch	**amerikanisch**	
biscuit	**cookie, cooky**	Keks
sweet	*candy*	Bonbon
jam	*jelly*	Marmelade
crisps	*potato chips*	Chips
chips	**(French) fries*	Pommes frites
trousers	*pants*	Hose
zip	*zipper*	Reißverschluß
shop	***store**	Geschäft
chemist's	*pharmacy*/**drugstore**	Apotheke
cinema	**movie theater**	Kino
go to the cinema	*go to the movies*	ins Kino gehen
film	**movie*	Film
bill	*check*	Rechnung (im Restaurant)
(bank)note	*bill*	Geldschein
handbag	**purse**	Handtasche
purse	**wallet** / *coin purse*	Portemonnaie
wallet	*billfold*	Brieftasche
petrol	*gas/gasoline*	Benzin
driving licence	**driver's license**	Führerschein
motorway	*highway/freeway/ expressway*	Autobahn
boot	*trunk*	Kofferraum
bonnet	*hood*	Kühlerhaube
windscreen	*windshield*	Windschutzscheibe
accelerator	*gas pedal*	Gaspedal
hire a car	*rent a car*	ein Auto mieten
taxi	**cab*	Taxi
railway	*railroad*	Bahn
rails	**tracks*	Gleis(e)
public transport	*public transportation*	öffentliche Verkehrsmittel
pavement	**sidewalk**	Bürgersteig
underground	**subway**	U-Bahn

---

* Diese Wörter werden Sie auch im britischen Englisch finden.

britisch	**amerikanisch**	
subway	*(pedestrian) underpass*	Fußgängerunterführung
queue	***line**	Schlange
city centre	downtown	City, Innenstadt
flat	apartment	Wohnung
ground floor	first floor	Erdgeschoß
lift	elevator	Aufzug
cloakroom	checkroom	Garderobe
cupboard	closet	Schrank
toilet	bathroom / rest room	W.C.
tap	faucet	Wasserhahn
nappy	diaper	Babywindel
torch	flashlight	Taschenlampe
rubbish	*garbage/trash	Abfall
rubber	*eraser	Radiergummi
timetable	*schedule	Fahrplan
postbox	mailbox	Briefkasten
parcel	***package**	Päckchen, Paket
send	***mail**	schicken
holiday	vacation	Urlaub
autumn	fall	Herbst
sorry	excuse me	Entschuldigung!
pardon?/sorry?	excuse me?	Wie bitte?
of course	***sure**	(Aber) Natürlich!

---

* *Diese Wörter werden Sie auch im britischen Englisch finden.*

„Falsche Freunde"

Wir alle kennen sie, die sogenannten „falschen Freunde": deutsche und englische Wörter, die auf den ersten Blick eng miteinander befreundet zu sein scheinen, in Wirklichkeit aber wenig miteinander zu tun haben, ja manchmal sogar das genaue Gegenteil ausdrücken können. Versuchen wir, ein paar der heimtückischsten zu demaskieren:

Angst haben

Some pupils <u>are scared</u> to go home with their school reports because they have such bad marks. Sometimes I feel quite anxious about these poor kids and the pressure their parents put them under.

be scared/frightened/afraid (of) – Angst haben (vor)

 be/feel anxious about – besorgt sein um

be anxious to – darauf bedacht sein zu

---

bekommen

All I <u>got</u> for the article I wrote was five free copies of the magazine. I'm not really sure whether I'm on the right road to becoming rich and famous.

get, be given, receive – bekommen

 become – werden (siehe auch **werden** im Hauptteil)

(sich) blamieren

"Whenever we go out together he always <u>makes a fool of himself</u>, and <u>shows me up</u> at the same time."
"Well, you only have yourself to blame – we all warned you against marrying him."

show s.o. (o.s.) up – jd. (sich) blamieren

make a fool of s.o. (o.s.) – jd. (sich) lächerlich machen

 blame s.o. – jdm. die Schuld geben

Brieftasche

I had put my <u>wallet</u> with all that money into my briefcase because you can lock it. Then, stupidly, I left my briefcase on the train.

wallet – Brieftasche

 briefcase – Aktentasche

Chips

"Do you remember the days when there used to be a little blue bag of salt in every packet of <u>crisps</u>?"
"Oh yes. And I also remember eating fish 'n' chips out of newspaper. Times have certainly changed."

crisps – (Kartoffel)Chips   [Am. *potato chips*]

 chips – Pommes frites   [Am. *(French) fries*]

---

engagiert

He used to be a very <u>committed</u> politician. But since he's been engaged to that fashion model he seems to have his mind on other things.

committed – engagiert
be very involved in politics – politisch engagiert sein

 engaged – **1.** verlobt;   **2.** (Telefon, Toilette) besetzt

eventuell

He says he <u>might possibly</u> be home by eight tonight, but he's always late. And even when he does eventually get back from work, he usually falls straight asleep on the sofa.

possibly – eventuell

"Will you do it?" – ***"I might."*** – ... „Eventuell."

I might consider doing it – ich würde es eventuell machen

 eventually – schließlich (= nach längerer Zeit/Mühe)

Karton

Could you fetch me one of those <u>cardboard boxes</u> from over there, please. I can't get all these cartons of milk into the shopping bag.

(cardboard) box, (kleiner) ***shoebox*** – Karton

 carton of milk – Milchtüte
carton of orange juice usw. – Packung Orangensaft usw.
carton of cigarettes – Stange Zigaretten

Menü

I don't really fancy the <u>set lunch</u>. I think I'd better have a look at the menu and order à la carte.

set meal, set lunch – Menü

 menu – Speisekarte

Note

See this fifty-pound note? If your <u>marks</u> in French and Geography improve by the end of term, it's yours.

mark /(bes. Am.) ***grade*** – Schulnote

 note – **1.** Geldschein [Am. *bill*]; **2.** Musiknote

Phantasie

Well, he's certainly got plenty of <u>imagination</u> – all these fantasies he has about writing a best-seller, getting rich and buying an island in the Pacific.

imagination – Phantasie, Vorstellungskraft

 fantasy – phantastische Vorstellung, Vision

 fantasy ist immer etwas <u>Phantastisches</u>

---

psychisch

Now she claims she's got psychic powers and can communicate with the dead. I know she's always had <u>psychological</u> problems, but if it goes on like this she'll end up as a <u>mental</u> case.

psychological – psychisch

mental – **1.** psychisch; **2.** geisteskrank

 psychic – übersinnliche Kräfte besitzend, hellseherisch

Rückseite

He's stuck the stamp on the <u>back</u> of the envelope! Sometimes I feel like giving him a kick in the backside.

back – Rückseite

 backside – Hintern

"I wrote it on the backside."

selbstbewußt

My new assistant's such a <u>self-confident</u> young lady and really knows what she's talking about. I have a feeling the others in the department feel quite self-conscious when she's around.

self-confident – selbstbewußt

 self-conscious – befangen, gehemmt, unsicher

---

sensibel

"Don't keep criticizing his English – he's very <u>sensitive</u>."
"Well, if he was sensible about it he'd spend more time with his books so that he wouldn't make so many mistakes."

sensitive – sensibel, empfindlich

 sensible – vernünftig

---

starten

"We'd better <u>set off</u> for the airport now if we want to catch our flight."
"Yes, I remember the last time we got to Heathrow just as our plane to Toronto was <u>taking off</u> ..."
"All right, let's not start that business again."

set off – starten, losfahren, abreisen

take off – (Flugzeug) starten

 start – beginnen (mit), anfangen (mit)

Studium

She takes her <u>studies</u> very seriously – she spends most of her time upstairs in her Dad's study buried in a pile of books.

(course of) studies, degree – Studium, Studiengang

a degree in physics – ein Physikstudium (usw.)

 study – 1. Arbeitszimmer; 2. spezifische Untersuchung; 3. Erforschung

sympathisch

Our new neighbour seems a very likeable sort of person. And he was very sympathetic when our dog died last week.

likeable, very pleasant, nice, personable – sympathisch

 sympathetic – 1. mitfühlend; 2. verständnisvoll

überhören

*"I missed that – did he say he was going into retirement?"
"I didn't catch it either, it's so noisy in here. But I did overhear him saying to Mark yesterday that he's had enough of this company."*

miss, not catch – überhören

 overhear – zufällig (mit)hören, mitbekommen, „aufschnappen"

übernehmen

When he takes over his father's company, he'll have overtaken us all on the income scale.

take over – übernehmen

 overtake – (auch im Verkehr) überholen

Unternehmer

He started off as an undertaker with a very small business. Now he's teamed up with a clever businessman and has himself become a successful entrepreneur with a worldwide market for exclusive animal coffins.

entrepreneur, (big) businessman – Unternehmer

industrialist – industrieller Unternehmer

 undertaker – Leichenbestatter

Warenhaus

I had hoped to be able to pick up a bookcase at the <u>department store</u>, but they had most of their furniture in the warehouse, so I had to drive all the way out of town to get it.

department store – Warenhaus

 warehouse – (Waren)Lager

---

sich wundern

I <u>was surprised</u> to see her with Tony all of a sudden. I wonder if she and Paul have broken up.

be surprised – sich wundern

 wonder – sich fragen

    I wonder if – ich würde ganz gern wissen, ob

Holen Sie noch einmal tief Luft: Es kommt nun der allerletzte, dafür etwas ausführlichere Test. Übersetzen Sie das Deutsche in Klammern:

1. Let me see what's written on the _____ (*Rückseite*) of that photo.

2. You have to watch what you say to her – she's very _____ (*sensibel*).

3. When are we going to _____ (*übernehmen*) this company and shake it up a bit?

4. "Are you coming to the reading by Salman Rushdie?" – "_____ (*eventuell*)."

5. What _____ (*Note*) did he get in English?

6. I need some strong _____ (*Kartons*) to pack all these books into.

7. He's the kind of model _____ (*Unternehmer*) Mrs Thatcher always used to praise.

8. Try not to _____ (*uns blamieren*) again this time.

9. If you haven't got a recipe for stew, just use your _____ (*Phantasie*).

10. Do you think you could crunch your _____ (*Chips*) a bit more quietly, please.

11. You really shouldn't keep both your cheque card and your cheques in your _____ (*Brieftasche*).

12. The _____ (*Menü*) looks quite interesting, and it's fairly cheap – shall we take that?

13. He's incompetent and thick, and yet he goes around with such a _____ (*selbstbewußt*) air.

14. A fire broke out at one of the _____ (*Warenhäuser*) in the pedestrian precinct last night.

15. The new head of personnel doesn't seem to be very _____ (*sympathisch*).

16. How much did you _____ (*bekommen*) for your Skoda?

17. What we need is more _____ (*engagiert*) employees who are prepared to do overtime.

18. A lot of the patients with severe _____ (*psychisch*) disorders started off with quite minor _____ (*psychisch*) problems.

19. I'm afraid I _____ (*überhörte*) most of the figures she was quoting.

20. After two _____ (*Studiengänge*), don't you think it's time you got down to some real work?

21. Everyone _____ (*hat sich gewundert*) to see me back from my skiing holiday so soon.

22. Why _____ (*hast du Angst*) to ask him?

23. The hijacked plane is due to _____ (*starten*) for Athens in half an hour.

Schlüssel zu den Übungen

A. Hauptteil

aufstehen: 1. get up; **2.** stand up
Bank: 1. bench; **2.** bank; **3.** benches
bemerken: she **noticed** me; she loudly **remarked**
bequem: 1. convenient; **2.** comfortable; **3.** lazy; easy; **4.** easy
besondere(r,-s): something **special**; one **particular** video camera; a **special** price
besuchen: 1. go to; **2.** attend; **3.** go and see; **4.** visit
bis (zu): 1. by; **2.** until; **3.** By the time
Boden: The **ground**; the living-room **floor**
brauchen: 1. I need a tie for the wedding. **2.** It only takes him ten minutes to type a page. **3.** How long did it take you to get here?
bringen: 1. took; **2.** bring/get; **3.** bring
Chef: 1. chef; **2.** boss
dick: much too **fat**; a **thick** book; that **thick**
eng: 1. cramped; **2.** close; **3.** tight; **4.** narrow
erkennen: 1. realize; **2.** recognize
erst: 1. Lunch won't be ready until two. **2.** The cheque only arrived the day before yesterday. **3.** He won't be fifty until next year. **4.** They've only won one game/match (so far).
fahren: going for; how to **travel**; **go** by train; like **driving**; **travel** long distances; be **driven** around
Fehler: a **fault**; so many **mistakes**; the **mistakes**; printing **errors**; a character **flaw**
fertig: 1. Have you **finished**; **2. Are** you **ready**; **3.** when you **have finished**; **4. Are** you **ready**
Frau: so many **women**; my **wife**; a really elegant **lady**; a very intelligent **woman**

153

Fremder: 1. stranger; **2.** foreigners; **3.** strangers

Freund(in): a new **boyfriend**; He's a **friend**; a steady **girlfriend**

früher: 1. We used to have three dogs. **2.** You never used to be so funny. **3.** In the past there were a lot more monarchies in Europe. / (In the past) There used to be a lot more monarchies in Europe.

Garderobe: 1. hallstand; **2.** cloakroom; **3.** dressing-room

glücklich: 1. happy; lucky; **2.** lucky; happy; **3.** lucky

groß: 1. big; **2.** large; great; **3.** tall

Haare: 1. hair; hairs; **2.** hair; **3.** hairs

hören: Listen!; **hear** that noise; **hear** a thing; **listen to** the late-night news; **hear** another word

kennenlernen: first **met**; **get to know** each other

klein: 1. little; **2.** small; **3.** small; **4.** little

kochen: 1. boil; **2.** making; **3.** cooked

kontrollieren: 1. check; control; **2.** control; **3.** checked; **4.** checked

krank: 1. ill; **2.** sick; **3.** ill; **4.** sick

Kritik: your **criticism**; their **reviews**

Kurve: 1. bends; **2.** curve; **3.** corners

Land: 1. country; **2.** Land; Land; **3.** countries; **4.** land; country

Landschaft: 1. landscape; **2.** countryside; **3.** scenery

lassen: 1. leave; **2.** let; **3.** leave; **4.** let

laut: 1. noisy; **2.** loud; noisy; **3.** loud

leicht: 1. slight; **2.** light; **3.** slight; **4.** easy

leihen: I **borrowed**; **lend** me; **lent** something; I **borrowed**

lernen: studying / revising again; I've been **revising**; I had to **learn** ; and **revise**; **learnt** much

lustig sein: 1. funny; **2.** fun; **3.** fun; funny

machen: 1. making; doing; **2.** do; do; **3.** go on; do; went on; do/take; taken

meinen: 1. think; **2.** mean; mean; think; **3.** think

merken: 1. notice; **2.** realize; **3.** noticed; realized

Müll: 1. waste; **2.** rubbish; **3.** refuse/rubbish

nächste(r,-s): the **nearest** oasis; the **next** acacia tree; the **next** oasis

in der Nähe (von): near the race track; house **nearby**; **near** there; **nearby** comprehensive school

Natur: 1. countryside; **2.** natural environment; **3.** nature; **4.** natural surroundings / natural environment

Paar: 1. couple; **2.** pair

passen (zu): **suits** you; **goes with** your hair; **matches** your beach towel; **fit** you

Pause: 1. interval; 2. breaks; 3. breaks

Platz: a **space**; their proper **place**; plenty of **room**

Reise: 1. trip; 2. journey; 3. trip; voyage

Rezept: 1. recipe; 2. prescription; 3. recipe

ruhig: Be **quiet**!; sit **still**; keep **calm**

sagen: 1. says; 2. told; 3. told; said

Salat: salad; lettuce

Schatten: 1. shadows; 2. shade

schwer: getting **hard**er; a **heavy** lorry; very **difficult**

See: 1. lake; 2. sea; 3. Lake

seit: **for** a long time; **since** 1981; **for** years; **since** he was 14; **since** the pub opened

so: **so** self-confident; **such** a lot; goes on **like this**

sportlich: an **athletic** person; some **sporting** / **sports** event; a **sporty** type; a bit more **sporting**

stören: 1. bother; disturb; 2. bother; 3. spoiling

Straße: 1. road; 2. street; 3. road; 4. street

streng: the **strict** schoolmaster; a **severe** expression; less **severe**; **strict** discipline

Technik: when it comes to **technical matters**; special **technique**; modern **technology**; the latest **technology**; electrical **engineering** degree

Termin: 1. deadline; 2. appointments; 3. date

tödlich: 1. lethal/deadly; 2. fatal; 3. deadly/fatal

tragen: 1. wear; carry; 2. wearing; 3. wear; carry

Treppe(n): 1. stairs; 2. steps; 3. stairs

Übung: 1. exercises; 2. practice; 3. exercise

verboten: 1. prohibited; 2. not allowed; 3. forbidden

während: 1. while; during; 2. During

wenn: 1. If; 2. when; 3. If

werden: 1. got; 2. went; got; 3. getting; get; 4. going; getting

wie: 1. What's your new cleaning lady like? 2. How's Simon? 3. What was Andrew's school report like? 4. How are you?

wissenschaftlich: 1. academic; 2. scientific; 3. scholarly

Zuschauer: 1. spectators; 2. viewers; 3. audience

Falsche Freunde

1. back; **2.** sensitive; **3.** take over; **4.** I might / Possibly; **5.** mark/ grade; **6.** boxes / cardboard boxes; **7.** businessman/ entrepreneur; **8.** show us up / make a fool of us; **9.** imagination; **10.** crisps; **11.** wallet; **12.** set lunch / set meal; **13.** self-confident; **14.** department stores; **15.** likeable/pleasant/nice/ personable; **16.** get; **17.** committed; **18.** mental; psychological; **19.** missed / didn't catch; **20.** degrees; **21.** was surprised; **22.** are you scared/frightened/afraid; **23.** take off

Register

academic 137
afraid 145
allowed 128
anxious 145
appointment 121
athletic 112
attend 17
audience 139

back 148
backside 148
bank 11
become 134, 145
bench 11
bend 62
big 49
blame 146
boil 56
borrow 73
boss 24
bother 113
box 147
boyfriend 42
break 92
briefcase 146
bring 23
businessman 150
by the time 19

calm 101
cardboard box 147
carry 124
carton 147
catch 150

chef 24
chief 25
chips 146
cloakroom 45
close 27
coat rack 45
comfortable 14
committed 146
control 58
convenient 14
cook 56
corner 62
country 64
countryside 66, 88
couple 89
course of studies 149
cramped 27
crisps 146
critic 61
criticism 61
curve 62

date 121
deadline 121
deadly 122
degree 149
department store 151
difficult 106
disturb 113
do 78
dressing-room 45
drive 32
during 130

easy 14, 71
engaged 146
engineering 119
entrepreneur 150
error 35
eventually 147
exercise 127

fantasy 148
fat 26
fatal 122
fault 35
finish 37
fit 91
flaw 35
flight (of stairs) 126
floor 21
football pitch 96
for 109
forbidden 128
foreigner 40
friend 42
frightened 145
fun 76
funny 76

garbage 84
get 23, 133, 145
get to know 53
get up 10
girlfriend 42
give 145
go 32, 133
go and see 17

157

go to 17
go with 91
grade 147
great 49
great big 50
ground 21
grow 134

hair 51
hairs 51
half time 93
hallstand 45
happy 47
hard 106
hear 52
heavy 106
how 135
humanities 138

if 131
ill 59
imagination 148
in the past 43
industrialist 150
intermission 93
interval 92
involved 146

journey 97

lady 39
lake 108
land 64
landscape 66
large 49
lazy 14
learn 74
leave 68
lend 73
let 68
lethal 122
lettuce 104
light 71
like this (that) 110
likeable 150
listen (to) 52
litter 84
little 55
loud 69
lucky 47

make 56, 78
make a fool of 146
mark 147
match 91
mean 80
meet 53
mental 148
menu 147
Miss (Ms) 40
miss 150
mistake 35
mortal 123
Mrs 40
Ms (Miss) 40

narrow 27
natural environment 88
natural sciences 138
natural surroundings 88
nature 88
near 86
nearby 86
nearest 85
need 22
next 85
nice 150
noisy 69
not until 31
note 147
notice 13, 81

only 31
overhear 150
overtake 150

pair 89
particular 15
past 43
pause 93
pay s.o. a visit 17
personable 150
place 94
pleasant 150
possibly 147
practice 127
prescription 99
prohibited 128
psychic 148
psychological 148

quiet 101

ready 37
realize 29, 81
receipt 100
receive 145
recipe 99
recognize 29
refuse 83
remark 13
research 138
researcher 138
review 61
reviewer 61
revise 74
ride 32
road 115
room 94
rubbish 83

salad 104
say 102
scared 145
scenery 66
scholarly 137
science(s) 138
scientific 137
sea 108
seat 96
self-confident 149
self-conscious 149
sensible 149
sensitive 149
set lunch 147
set meal 147
set off 149
severe 117
shade 105
shadow 105
shoebox 147
show up 146
sick 59
since 109
slight 71
small 55
so 110
space 94
special 15
spectators 139
spoil 113
sporting 112

sports 112
sporty 112
square 96
stairs 126
stand up 10
start 149
steps 126
still 101
stranger 40
street 115
strict 117
studies 149
study 74, 149
such 110
surprised 151
sympathetic 150

take 22, 23, 78
take off 149

take over 150
tall 49
technical matters 119
technique 119
technology 119
tell 102
thick 26
think 80
tight 27
till 19
tour 98
tourist 41
trash 84
travel 32
trip 97

undertaker 150
until 19

used to 43

viewer 139
visit 17
voyage 97

wallet 146
wardrobe 45
warehouse 151
waste 83
wear 124
what ... like 135
when 131
while 130
wife 39
woman 39
wonder 151
write-up 61

humboldt BÜCHER, DIE ZUR SACHE KOMMEN!

Die aktuellen, illustrierten und praktischen Humboldt-Taschenbücher bieten in sieben Themengruppen ein umfassendes Programm:
Praktische Ratgeber, Kochen, Freizeit-Hobby-Quiz, Sport, Sprachen, Reisen, Moderne Information.
Eine Auswahl der Titel stellen wir Ihnen vor. Bandnummer in Klammern.

Praktische Ratgeber

Haushalt
Partybuch (231)
Kaufberater Biokost (608)
1000 Ideen für fröhliche Feste (623)
Haushaltsreparaturen selber machen (635)
Umweltschutz (642)
Schutz vor Einbruch, Diebstahl (663)
Ratgeber Privatversicherungen (678)

Getränke
Mixgetränke (218)
Alkoholfreie Mixgetränke (396)

Kind und Erziehung
Vornamen (210)
Unser Baby (233)
Schwangerschaft/Geburt (392)
Schwangerschafts-Gymnastik (468)
Gymnastik für Baby + Kleinkind (602)
Ich werde Vater (622)
Kinderspiele für unterwegs (631)
Kinderfeste (657)

Tips für Kinder
Kinderspiele (47)
Was Kinder basteln (172)
Was Kinder gerne raten (193)

Gesundheit
Erste Hilfe (207)
Kneippkur (230)
Autogenes Training (336)
Rückenschmerzen (339)
Guter Schlaf (354)
Rheuma (364)
Allergien (365)
Sauna (406)
Heilfasten (407)
Kopfschmerzen (408)
Entspannungs-Training (430)
Depressionen (431)
Bandscheibenbeschwerden (442)
Schluß mit dem Rauchen! (452)
Selbsthilfe durch Autogenes Training (466)
Kranke Seele (484)
Biorhythmus (494)
Autogenes Training und Meditation (510)
Chinesische Atem- und Heilgymnastik (519)
Homöopathie (553)
Erfolgsgeheimnis Selbsthypnose (571)
Schluß mit dem Rauchen! (572)
Ernährungsratgeber (586)
Ratgeber Wechseljahre (589)
Rezeptfreie Medikamente (593)
Aktiv gegen den Krebs (598)

Ratgeber Heuschnupfen (605)
Abwehrkräfte stärken (616)
Ratgeber Kinderkrankheiten (619)
Aktiv gegen Bluthochdruck (632)
Wassergymnastik (633)
Aktiv gegen Zellulitis (640)
Gymnastik bei Bandscheibenschäden (647)
Ärztl. Ratgeber für die Reise (655)
Ratgeber Hormone (658)
Humboldt-Nährwertplaner (659)
Gesunde und schöne Zähne (661)
Aktiv gegen Herzinfarkt (670)
Gesundheitsratgeber Cholesterin (671)
Schluß mit dem Diät-Streß! (674)
Gesunde und schöne Beine (675)
Gesund durch Entschlacken (676)

Schönheit
Welche Farben stehen mir? (577)
Schöner durch Naturkosmetik (648)
Alles über Schönheitsoperationen (686)

Praktische Lebenshilfe
So lernt man leichter! (191)
Traumbuch (226)
Reden f. jeden Anlaß (247)
Handschriften deuten (274)
Gästebuch (287)
Gutes Benehmen (303)
Gedächtnis-Training (313)
Superlearning (491)
Testament und Nachlaß (514)
Hochzeitsratgeber (529)
Prüfe Deine Menschenkenntnis (531)
Mietrecht knapp + klar (532)
Schlank werden (550)
Yoga für Frauen (588)
Körpersprache verstehen (590)
Das korrekte Testament (594)
Weniger Steuern zahlen (595)
Flirten – aber wie? (606)
Selbstsicher – selbstbewußt (609)
Teste deine Allgemeinbildung (618)
Positiv denken und leben (622)
Rhetorik (627)
Mein Geld (636)
Gutes Gedächtnis (639)
Trennung positiv bewältigen (644)
Geliebt werden – aber wie? (654)
Endlich 50! (657)
Bleib cool! (660)*
Linkshändig? (669)
Besser konzentrieren (672)
Besser lesen, verstehen, behalten (673)
Kommunikation (682)
Okkultismus (687)
Ich zieh' aus! (688)
Gesund wohnen (689)

Computer
BASIC Anfänger (456)
BASIC Fortgeschrittene (496)
Lernen mit dem Homecomputer (525)
Spielend Programmieren (526)
Programmiersprache PASCAL (551)
Bausteine für BASIC-Programme (591)
Computer-1×1 fürs Büro (638)

Briefe schreiben
Geschäftsbriefe (229)
Komma-Lexikon (259)
Briefe besser schreiben (301)
Liebesbriefe schreiben (297)
Gutes Deutsch – der Schlüssel zum Erfolg! (535)
Musterbriefe für den persönlichen Bereich (538)
Dichten und Reimen (545)
Fehlerfrei schreiben (615)

Beruf
Buchführung (211)
So bewirbt man sich (255)
Eignungstests (463)
Existenzgründung (498)
Sich bewerben und vorstellen (537)
Eignungs- und Persönlichkeitstests (548)
Arbeitszeugnisse (573)
Prüfungen mit Erfolg! (582)
Behörden-Wegweiser (592)
Arbeitslos – was nun? (597)
Berufe mit Zukunft (604)
Erfolg ist trainierbar (614)
Erfolgsgeheimnis Zeiteinteilung (624)
Jeder kann Karriere machen (641)
Tests für die Berufswahl (643)
Vom Umgang mit Chefs und Kollegen (662)
Die perfekte Bewerbung! (665)
Rückkehr ins Berufsleben (680)
Frauen im Beruf (681)
Alles über Computerberufe (685)

Zimmerpflanzen/Blumen
Zimmerpflanzen (270)
Die schönsten Zimmerpfl. (428)
Zimmerpflanzen selbst ziehen (585)

Haustiere
Katzen (212)
Schäferhunde (298)
Wie erziehe ich m. Hund (371)
Aquarienfische (447)
Meine Wohnungskatze (536)
Was will meine Katze mir sagen? (557)
Meine kranke Katze (611)

Sprachen

Englisch
Englisch in 30 Tagen (11)*
Englisch für Fortgeschr. (61)*
Englisch – Bild für Bild (296)
Englisch – jetzt in Comics (578)
Englischer Basis-Wortschatz (574)
Englische Grammatik (617)
Schluß mit typischen Englisch-Fehlern! (664)

Französisch
Französisch in 30 Tagen (40)*

Französisch für Fortgeschr. (109)
Französisch – Bild für Bild (344)
Französisch – jetzt in Comics (579)

Spanisch
Spanisch in 30 Tagen (57)*
Spanisch – Bild für Bild (345)
Spanisch – jetzt in Comics (579)
Spanisch für Fortgeschr. (626)*

Italienisch
Italienisch in 30 Tagen (55)*

Italienisch für Fortgeschr. (108)
Italienisch – Bild für Bild (344)
Italienisch – jetzt in Comics (580)

Weitere Sprachen
Russisch in 20 Lektionen (81)
Dänisch in 30 Tagen (124)
Griechisch für den Urlaub (373)
Griechisch – jetzt in Comics (652)
Türkisch für den Urlaub (628)*
Türkisch – jetzt in Comics (653)

Die mit * versehenen Titel gibt es auch als Buch **mit Übungscassette:** Englisch (800, 805), Französisch (801), Italienisch (802), Spanisch (803, 806), Türkisch (804), Bleib cool! (807)

HUMBOLDT-TASCHENBUCHVERLAG · MÜNCHEN